sew me!

sewing home décor

sew me!

sewing home décor

Easy-to-Make Curtains, Pillows, Organizers, and Other Accessories

Choly Knight

Design Originals

an Imprint of Fox Chapel Publishing
www.d-originals.com

ACQUISITION EDITOR
Peg Couch

COPY EDITOR
Colleen Dorsey

COVER AND PAGE DESIGNER
Lindsay Hess

COVER AND PROJECT PHOTOGRAPHER
Scott Kriner

EDITOR
Katie Weeber

LAYOUT DESIGNER
Maura J. Zimmer

ISBN 978-1-57421-504-5

Library of Congress Cataloging-in-Publication Data

Knight, Choly.
    Sew me! sewing home décor : easy-to-make curtains, pillows, organizers, and other accessories / Choly Knight.
        pages cm
    Includes index.
    ISBN 978-1-57421-504-5
    1. Sewing. 2. Household linens. 3. House furnishings. I. Title.
    TT705.K54 2013
    646.2'1--dc23
                        2013004464

© 2013 by Choly Knight and Design Originals, www.d-originals.com, an imprint of Fox Chapel Publishing, 800-457-9112,
1970 Broad Street, East Petersburg, PA 17520.

Printed in China
First printing

About the Author

Choly Knight is from Orlando, Florida, and is the author of *Sew Kawaii!*, *Sew Baby*, *Sewing Stylish Handbags*, and *Sew Me! Sewing Basics*. She has been crafting for as long as she can remember, and has drawn, painted, sculpted, and stitched everything in sight. She began sewing clothing in 1997 and has yet to put her sewing machine away. After studying studio art and earning a BA in English, she now enjoys trying to find numerous different ways to combine her passions for writing, fine art, and craft art. She created all of the designs, projects, and patterns that appear in this book. She focuses on handcrafted clothing, accessories, and other creations inspired by Japanese art, anime, and style, and specializes in cosplay (costume play) hats and hoodies. You can find out more about her and her work on her website: *www.cholyknight.com*.

Author Choly Knight

Contents

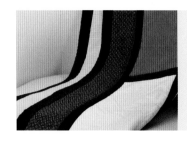

Make Your Space Your Own!

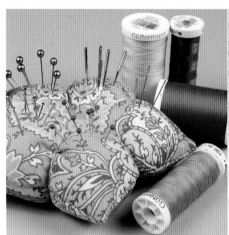

25 Build your basic sewing kit.

14 Select the perfect fabric for each project.

22 Learn how to laminate items and fuse plastic bags to create your own unique sewable fabric.

31 Refresh your memory on the basic techniques.

31 Review the standard machine stitches.

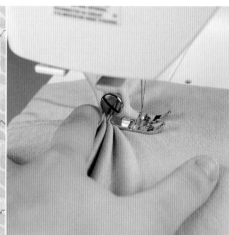

36 Get tips for working with tricky knit fabrics.

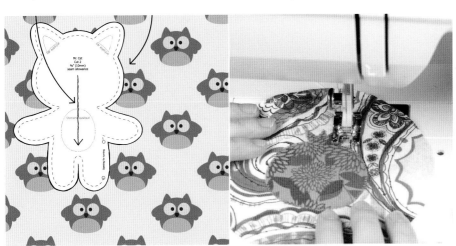

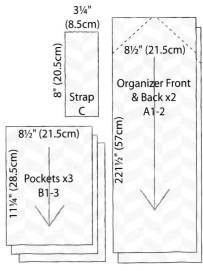

43 Understand how to work with patterns.

39 Learn how to enhance a project with appliqué.

48 Discover charts and diagrams to walk you through the prep work.

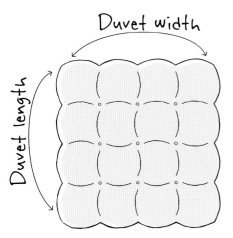

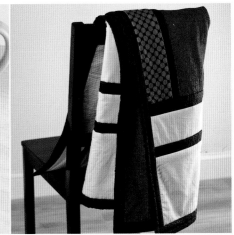

58 Take measurement to create projects that fit your exact needs.

48 Start with simple, quick projects.

78 Tackle ambitious projects as your skills improve!

Introduction

If you've picked up this book, then something about sewing home décor projects has gotten you excited. Maybe you dream of making designer home furnishings worthy of the most elite interior decorators, have an empty apartment in need of creative colors and soft surroundings, have a new sewing machine and want to know how to make it work for you, or simply want to treat yourself and those closest to you to handmade treasures. But with all those lofty ideas in the future, it can seem daunting to take that first step and get going.

I, too, was intimidated by the task of threading the needle. It's hard not to feel scared when setting out to sew your own home accents for the first time. What finally convinced me it was worthwhile was my first Home Economics class in middle school. Seeing how a few simple yards of cotton could be transformed into a useful item made me realize the limitless possibilities sewing had. The machine, shears, and needles were only tools—I just had to find out what made them tick and they were mine to control, not to fear.

I know you will feel the same way when you discover all the techniques and tools you can use to create beautiful home décor projects that perfectly suit your personal taste. Ruffles, quilting, appliqué, grommets, and interfacing are like paints on your palette, ready to be used on the canvas. And you really can't beat the feeling of making something from nothing—taking plain fabric and turning it into something useful and beautiful with just your two hands and a sewing machine. Soon, you'll begin to see raw materials in a whole new light. An old button-down shirt can become a clever buttoned pillow cover; old scraps of paper can be sewn into a handy letter caddy. Your whole perspective will change when you begin to see the opportunities.

Despite the kind of creativity you can feel while sewing, people often ask me why I bother. Why go through the trouble of sewing when extremely cheap home furnishings can be found just about anywhere? It's true, the cheapest home décor on the market can't compare with the cost of sewing for yourself, but there are lots of other reasons to take sewing into your own hands.

Sewing gives you tons of options, like creating a lap quilt to snuggle up in while you read a book or watch your favorite movie. Sewing this project yourself means you can pick colors to match your dorm or apartment décor, and you can pick your favorite snuggly fabric, from fleece to minky to cotton.

After I got the taste of thread and fabric, I realized I didn't have to settle any longer. It's strangely perfect that I learned to sew at the age that I was, because I was already excited about developing my own sense of taste, style, and individuality. Sewing helped me unlock those things to their full potential. While doing my oh-so-important dorm shopping, I could (almost defiantly) say that, no, I didn't like this season's colors! And no, I wasn't going to fill my closet with mothball scented thrift-store blankets. I would just make a quilt of my own!

Over the years I developed a very specific taste that could only be satisfied by intense and arduous retail shopping trips or a single, easy trip to the fabric store. My history with arts and crafts makes my taste a little quirky, and I find I'm always disappointed by the selection of goods at everyday stores. Sewing is how I know I can get exactly what I want—that I can cover my windows with curtains in the exact colors that cheer me up the most, or can wrap myself in blankets with the fabrics I know will comfort me the best. I encourage all of you would-be sewers out there with an eccentric or particular sense of style to pick up your needles, if only for this reason. In the end, making things yourself

ensures your home décor will be truly unique, and you've probably paid much less for that custom look!

This brings back the original argument, is sewing really cheaper than buying? For bargain-basement wares, sure: bed sheets, plain pillowcases, bath towels. Basics that wear out after a year of use are nearly impossible to beat pricewise, but suppose you want something more high-end? A trendy throw pillow or a luxurious lap quilt? You'll see the prices jump for these items, though the quality of materials and construction might be exactly the same as their cheaper counterparts. If you shop for the right fabrics at the right time, you can easily purchase exactly what you need for half the price of the finished product at a department store.

Not having to pay someone else for labor is the boon here. If you're making it yourself, you'll know the construction is much better than what you would get from a factory that rushes hundreds of units a day, so your project will last longer too! It's true, the cost of tools and notions is pricey at first, but if you keep sewing, then the investment in tools you'll use for years will save you more and more money in the long run.

With all of this in mind, you'll learn that sewing doesn't have to be scary, restricting, or expensive. You can see how your tools will work for you to achieve whatever you can imagine, whether it's unique, creative, or frugal. Yes, there will be headaches and there will be mistakes, but if you're willing to try, you'll see at most they will result in some stitches to rip and a bit of fabric wasted. No amount of frustration can compare with the feeling of creating your own one-of-a-kind home décor pieces, and this book will help to take you on that fabulous journey!

Every home can use a bit of organization, and there are plenty of storage cubes and shelves available for sale. But the storage boxes you find in the store will never have the same personality as ones you make yourself. These storage boxes can be customized to the exact size you want, with colors you love and appliqué you adore!

Getting Started

The projects in this book require some very basic sewing techniques, so if you are familiar with sewing you can look through this section to get refreshed on the basic skills you'll be using. If you're not so familiar with sewing, however, this chapter is great to get you acquainted with some indispensible information about skills, techniques, and fabrics. For more information, check out *Sew Me! Sewing Basics*.

This chapter will also give you information about the projects, which are ranked by difficulty, taking into account the time required and complexity of the techniques used. If you want to get the most out of this book, start with the very easy projects and work your way up. You'll find that as your skills increase, you'll be able to tackle more and more difficult projects until your entire home is decorated!

Fabrics

Purchasing fabric for a project is always an exciting process, and with a little bit of knowledge going in, you can ensure your trip to the fabric store is a creative adventure instead of an arduous process. Picking the right fabric can help you make a project you'll want to keep forever. Here's everything you need to know about finding and buying fabric so you're sure to be happy with your purchase.

The best way to categorize fabrics so you make the right choice is to divide them between fabrics that stretch and fabrics that don't. These are called wovens and knits. Beyond that, they are broken down by thickness or weight. If you learn to see fabric in this way, you can be sure to get the best fabric for the job.

WOVEN FABRICS

Woven fabrics are the kind that should come to mind when you think of your favorite button-down shirt, a sturdy tote bag, or a fancy pair of slacks. These fabrics are made by weaving threads together, just like basket pieces, to form the fabric. They can be made from synthetic or natural fibers and range from large weaves like burlap to delicate weaves like fine silk.

Wovens: Woven fabrics are made just like a basket, but on a much smaller scale. They're sturdy and reliable, but have the unfortunate quality of unraveling as the threads gradually pull away at the edges.

About Metric

Throughout this book, you'll notice that every measurement is accompanied by a metric equivalent. Inches and yards are rounded off to the nearest half or whole centimeter unless precision is necessary. Please be aware that while this book will show 1 yard = 100 centimeters, the actual conversion is 1 yard = 90 centimeters, a difference of about 3^{15}⁄₁₆" (10cm). Using these conversions, you will always have a little bit of extra fabric if purchasing by the metric quantity.

Lightweight wovens

Lightweight woven fabrics encompass some very reliable and versatile fabrics that are perfect for beginners. Lightweight fabrics tend to bend and twist more easily for what you are trying to sew and are more accommodating to your projects. If your project has curves, ruffles, or intricate shapes, stick with a lightweight fabric.

Quilting cotton: It doesn't get more reliable than quilting cotton. Although this fabric is meant for quilts, it can be used for accessories and clothing as well. In fact, just about every project in this book can be made from quilting cotton. It's sturdy, behaves predictably, irons beautifully, and is perfect for beginners. You can find it in a multitude of designs and it even gets softer with every wash. Solid varieties of this cotton are called broadcloth, and versions woven with a smooth, shiny finish are called sateen cotton.

Flannel: Flannel is like the softer cousin of quilting cotton. It's still just as reliable but has a slightly fuzzy, brushed feel to it.

Shirting: This is an umbrella term used to describe fabrics that work well for shirts. They are typically made from synthetic fibers or blends, and can range in texture from smooth like quilting cotton and fluffy like flannel to puckered textures like gauze, gingham, and seersucker. They sew similarly to cotton, except they are less stiff and therefore work better for shirts.

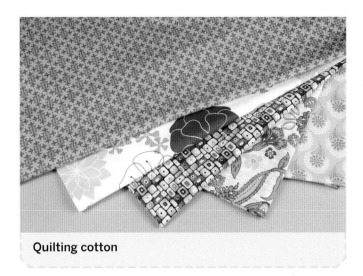

Quilting cotton

Flannel

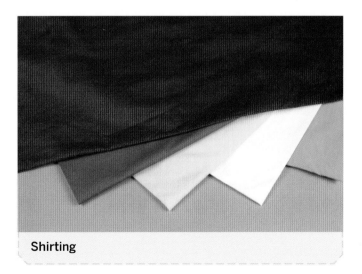

Shirting

Silk & satin: Satin and similar fabrics are typically made from synthetic fibers and have a quality that's often called "slinky" or "drapey." If you pinch the middle of the fabric and hold it up, you'll see that the surrounding fabric drapes completely with almost no stiffness. This drapey quality, in addition to the beautiful sheen, is what makes satin such a luxury. Unfortunately, this is also what makes satin move so unpredictably while you sew. It takes a bit of practice to get used to satin, so start out with small projects after you've honed your skills with more stable fabrics.

Silk & satin

Medium-weight wovens

Medium-weight fabrics can't conform to as many shapes and details as lighter-weight fabrics, but they make up for it in being heftier and great for taking on tougher tasks.

Linen: Linen is a similar fabric to cotton, being very easy to work with and reliable. It's made from a natural fiber (flax), though synthetic blends are very common and can change the feel of the fabric. It's associated with the noticeable woven fibers that run through it, and it often has a drapey quality.

Twill & denim: Twill is a kind of woven fabric that is defined by the diagonal weave present in the fabric texture (so denim is a kind of twill). However, it can best be described as the fabric used for khaki pants or light jackets. It is often made from cotton, although stretchable synthetics and blends are common. It sews very predictably, though its thickness makes it a little less forgiving. Fabrics similar to twill are often found with the name bottomweights.

Linen

Twill

Corduroy: Corduroy is a fabric similar to twill that has raised "cords" with a velvet-like texture. It sews up nicely, although care must be taken that the cords run in the right direction in the finished product. This is called the nap, and means the direction where stroking the fabric feels smooth and natural (like an animal's coat). Various prints and colors are becoming popular with this fabric, which would make it great for pillow covers and throws.

Brocade: Brocade is a kind of satin with layers of embroidery in the woven fabric. It's much more stable than its thinner cousins, so although sewing with satin can be tricky, brocades can be rather kind to beginners by comparison. Besides that, it's hard to turn down all those gorgeous colors and patterns.

Suiting: Suiting fabric is a bit of an umbrella term to cover fabrics that work well in making suits. They're typically made from combinations of wool, polyester, and rayon and come in sophisticated and classic colors and prints.

Corduroy

Brocade

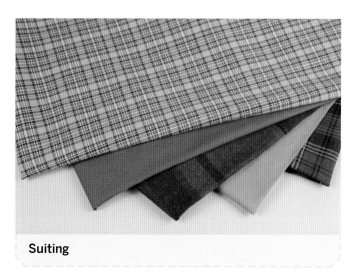

Suiting

Heavyweight wovens

The average person typically encounters heavyweight fabrics through furniture and home textiles. Fabrics like these work better on a large scale, or if not that, at least with straight, simple lines with few curves and corners. So while heavyweight fabrics are typically harder to work with, here are some suggestions that should encourage you to experiment.

Canvas: Typically made from cotton or linen, canvas is a thick fabric with a very large weave. It tends to be stiff and difficult to sew through, but with the right sewing needle, the results are strong and sturdy. It is also known as cotton duck.

Home décor fabrics: This is an umbrella term that covers various thick and printed varieties of fabrics for window dressings and upholstery. Smooth solid and printed varieties of twill and canvas work nicely for curtains and pillows. However, heavily embroidered and plush varieties can overcomplicate your project and make sewing difficult, so steer clear of those until you've had more practice with simpler fabrics.

Faux suede: This fabric is a bit of a guilty pleasure for me, and I snatch it up whenever I find it. The texture is wonderful and the range of colors available is amazing. This suede substitute is made from adhering a suede-like nap onto a woven fabric. It sews very well, though ironing can sometimes damage the surface. At stores it might also be called suedecloth or ultrasuede.

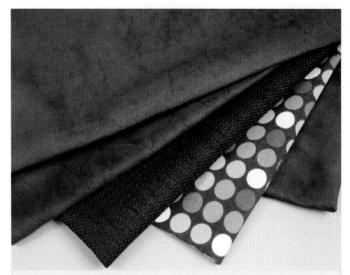

Heavyweight fabrics: Fabrics like canvas, simple home décor fabrics, and faux suede are great heavyweights for beginners.

KNIT FABRICS

Knit fabrics are constructed differently from woven fabrics in that they are created by knitting threads to form the fabric. This is similar to the way a sweater is made (but on a much smaller scale) and exactly what you find in your favorite t-shirts. Knit fabrics are special in that they stretch, usually horizontally along the fabric, but sometimes both horizontally and vertically. Because of this, knits are typically used for clothing and wearable accessories because they conform to the shape of the body. Sewing knits is a bit of a challenge all its own, so tips for sewing with knits can be found later in the book (page 36).

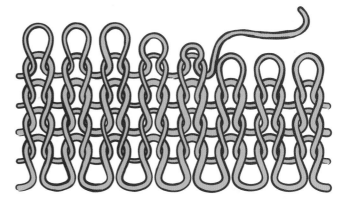

Knit fabrics: Threads are knitted together to create knit fabrics, which have the wonderful quality of stretching to fit snugly but not unraveling.

Lightweight knits

Jersey: This is the name to look for when you consider a thin t-shirt fabric. It's manufactured with a right side (the flat, or knit side if you are a knitter) and a wrong side (the piled or purl side). It is extremely stretchy along the horizontal axis, which can make it tricky to sew, but results in a very lovely drape. It comes in cotton and synthetic blends and is sometimes called single knit.

Lycra/spandex: These fabrics are similar to jersey in their weight, yet they are made from synthetic materials like polyester, nylon, rayon, and Lycra. They sometimes stretch in four directions, making fit easier. This is what's used to make swimsuits and leotards, and can make for some very interesting pillows for when your skills progress!

Jersey

Lycra & spandex

Medium-weight knits

Interlock: This fabric is knitted in the same way as jersey, but it is knitted in two layers so both sides are finished to look smooth. Because the fabric is thicker, it doesn't stretch nearly as much, so there's less drape, but it's also somewhat easier to work with. This fabric comes in a great abundance of natural fibers and synthetic blends.

Fleece: Fleece is a polyester fabric with a soft nap knitted into the base of the textile. This popular fabric can be seen in a lot of store-bought jackets, hats, and mittens and sews very easily for beginners. While it stretches enough to fit well, the stretchiness doesn't affect how it sews, so I can't recommend it enough for all your warm and fluffy projects. It's also available in a plethora of solid colors and prints.

Minky: Minky is a kind of faux fur similar in construction to fleece. The feel, however, is remarkably soft and delightful. It comes in lots of bright colors and piles, from short and smooth to shaggy and long to novelty designs like diamonds and stripes.

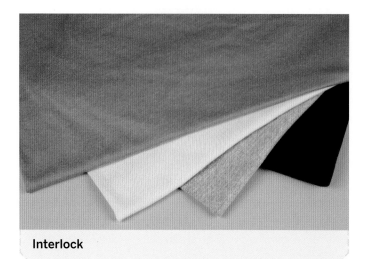

Interlock

Fleece

Minky

ADDITIONAL OPTIONS

Felt: Set slightly apart from other fabrics, felt is typically thought of more for crafting and accessories. Its fibers are neither woven nor knit, but rather intensely compressed to form a sheet. Because of this, using high-quality woolen felt is always best, as the fibers will be less likely to separate over time. And because felt does not fray, it is perfect for tiny embellishments and details.

Terry cloth: Terry cloth is a fabric that really works double time. Many new varieties are extremely soft and colorful. Cut-up towels work beautifully as a substitute, and using a bit of terry cloth for appliqué or other small touches can add a unique look and feel to a project.

Vinyl & faux leather: Vinyl and faux leather are heavyweight fabrics that act more like plastic. They have great strength and durability, but are often difficult to work with because they don't run through the machine easily. A lightweight stabilizer can help with this; see the Sewing Tools section (page 25) for more information. Also be sure to use a sewing machine needle specifically for vinyl or leather when sewing with these fabrics.

Felt

Terry cloth

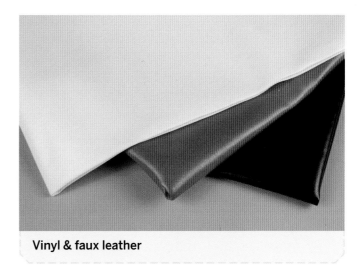

Vinyl & faux leather

Recycled materials: See below for information on how to melt and reuse plastic bags for sewing and also how to laminate items with iron-on vinyl for sewing. Anything from grocery bags, food bags, old books, artwork, and even gift-wrapping paper will work! These materials will act very similarly to vinyl and faux leather and will require a needle for vinyl to sew properly.

Recycled materials

Found fabrics: You'll find a great resource for project supplies at thrift stores or anywhere else used items are sold. Old pants or jackets make for wonderfully sturdy fabric and old dresses are nice for lining or creating a fancier look. Even better are the bits of old hardware you can find on old bags and luggage.

Found fabrics

FUSING PLASTIC BAGS INTO SEWABLE FABRIC

Grocery store bags only ever seem to have one or two uses in them before they start falling apart. Why not make them more durable by fusing several bags together into a thick sheet? This sheet is then sewable, and you can use it to make any number of projects. To make one sheet, gather up about three to four grocery bags and large sheets of parchment paper. Also make sure to open your windows and get plenty of ventilation in case some unwelcome fumes start to come off the plastic.

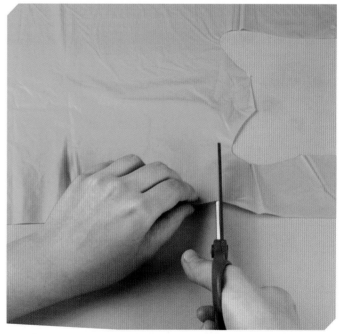

1 **Trim the bags.** Flatten and smooth out the bags, and then trim off the handles and bottom seam. You should be left with a smooth sheet of plastic that forms a tube.

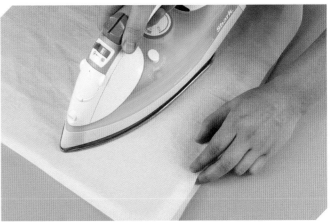

2 **Layer the plastic between the paper.** Layer the tube of plastic between the sheets of parchment paper. If your bag has writing on it, turn it inside out so the ink doesn't melt onto the parchment paper.

3 **Iron the plastic.** Using a medium-low setting on the iron and with the steam turned off, iron over the sheet of parchment paper to meld the plastic together. Run the iron smoothly and evenly over the paper for about thirty seconds until the pieces are fused.

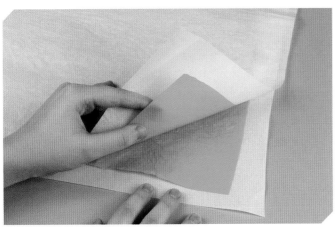

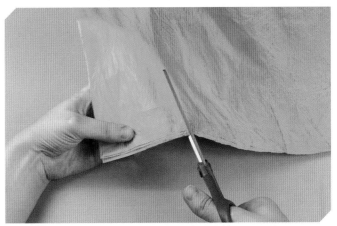

4 **Add more plastic.** Allow the plastic to cool completely and peel the parchment paper off. Add more sheets of plastic and repeat Step 3 until you have a 6-ply sheet. An 8-ply sheet would also work well if your bags are especially thin or you want a stronger, thicker project.

5 **Finish and use the sheet.** After several repetitions of Step 3, you'll have a sturdy sheet of plastic that is ready to sew. You can cut it with scissors or a craft knife to the shape you need, and it won't unravel like fabric. Be sure to use a needle intended for vinyl when sewing with it.

Not all plastic is created equal

Each plastic bag can be different, so it helps to experiment first when ironing your bags. Use the scraps from the handles if necessary to see how your plastic reacts to different heat settings. When fusing the bags, there's a sweet spot that is the goal. The plastic should get hot enough to melt, but not so hot that it warps, shrinks, or forms holes. Experiment with different heat settings and how fast you move the iron.

When you check your fused plastic, shallow wrinkles are completely normal. However, deep wrinkles are a sign that the iron may have been too hot, so try to go cooler next time. Bubbles are a sign that the plastic didn't get hot enough to fuse completely. These can be weak points and should be ironed again.

LAMINATING MEDIA WITH IRON-ON VINYL

In addition to melting plastic bags, you can make your own vinyl fabric from collected media and iron-on vinyl. Gather up any interesting flat media like food wrappers, photos, newspapers, or even items you've collaged yourself, and laminate them with iron-on vinyl. The result can be used to make any project that is suitable for vinyl and faux leather—all with fabric you designed!

1 **Prepare the medium.** Prepare the item you wish to laminate by making sure it is trimmed of unwanted parts and is entirely smooth, flat, and clean. Lay it on a larger piece of parchment paper.

2 **Layer the sheets.** Apply the adhesive side of the iron-on vinyl to the right side of your medium. Sandwich this between two sheets of parchment paper.

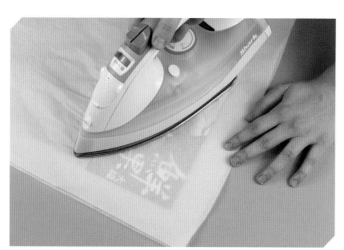

3 **Iron the vinyl.** Iron the vinyl to the medium following the manufacturer's instructions. After cooling, the vinyl should be completely adhered to the medium. Repeat Steps 2–3 for the other side of the medium.

4 **Prepare the piece for sewing.** Trim away the excess vinyl and use the piece to cut out your pattern. It can be cut with scissors or a craft knife and sewn with a needle suitable for vinyl or faux leather.

Sewing Tools

You can get through just about any project in this book with the most basic sewing tools one would usually have in a sewing kit. Some other, more specialty, tools are useful to have to make the process easier and quicker, so look through them here if you feel like you want to add them to your arsenal.

BASIC SEWING KIT

Sewing machine: Check out the book *Sew Me! Sewing Basics* to learn how to buy and what to look for in a great sewing machine that you can rely on for years to come.

Sewing shears: Unlike regular scissors, sewing shears are much sharper and, when taken care of properly, can cut through fabric like butter. Avoid cutting paper with them because this will dull the blade quickly.

You don't have to go expensive to get the job done, but the more expensive, higher-quality shears can last a lifetime (with sharpening) and are ideal if you want to sew further down the line.

Craft scissors: A typical pair of comfortable scissors work fine as craft scissors. Use these to cut paper patterns, thread, or any other material that would dull sewing shears.

Sewing shears are essential for every sewing project. Large sewing shears are best for cutting large pieces of fabric down to the appropriate dimensions, but you can also purchase medium and small shears for trimming smaller pieces of fabric and thread. Always take good care of your sewing shears and they'll stay sharp through many projects. Even an inexpensive pair will cut much better than anything in your junk drawer.

Tape measure or ruler: Sewing doesn't have to be an exact science, but it's good to have a ruler around so you know you are accurately making your project to the size you want. A tape measure is a necessity when sewing clothes or other large projects. You'll want the flexible fabric kind; they're extremely cheap, so it doesn't hurt to have more than one if the sewing bug has really bit you. For rulers, a yardstick often does the trick, but if you're willing to spend the extra money on a transparent quilting ruler you'll find it's very helpful for cutting pattern pieces.

Seam ripper: This strange-looking tool is for picking out and cutting stitches in seams you'd like to undo. Even the best of us make mistakes, so don't be afraid to use one.

Iron: Ironing is really crucial for professional-looking results in projects made with crisp fabrics such as cotton, twill, and the like. Even a cheap iron can do the job, but more expensive irons are a good investment if you plan to sew for years. Higher-quality irons are heavier (to make pressing and creasing easier), have more precise heat settings, and also have steam and spray functions.

Fabric marker: If there's one little tool that will save you from sewing headaches, it has to be the fabric marker. These pens are made with disappearing (or water-soluble) ink that can be used to draw on your fabric. You can use these to mark places for buttons, zippers, pockets, or anything else that needs to be matched up on your main fabric. You might think it's unnecessary, but you'd be surprised how a little mark can go a long way. Consider getting a light-colored pencil for dark fabrics and a dark marker for light fabrics.

Carbon tracing paper & wheel: An alternative to fabric markers is carbon tracing paper and a tracing wheel. First, the carbon paper and fabric are stacked, and then the wheel is run along the pattern guidelines. This transfers carbon marks to the fabric, which can be washed away later.

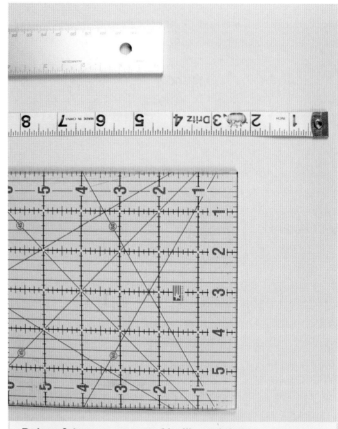

Rulers & tape measures: You'll need these to measure accurate cuts in your fabric.

Seam ripper & fabric marker: Little tools that make a world of difference!

Sewing pins: These little guys are used for temporarily holding pieces of fabric together while you sew. They come in different lengths and degrees of sharpness, but beginners should be more comfortable with larger, longer pins with big plastic heads. They sometimes leave slightly noticeable holes in your fabric, but you can work your way up to smaller, less obtrusive pins as you get comfortable.

Sewing machine needle: Your sewing machine needs a special kind of needle that fits specifically into your machine. They are made to suit different thicknesses of fabric in both knit and woven varieties. They are assigned a number between 8 and 19 (American) or 60 and 120 (European), with the low numbers in the range for light fabrics and the higher numbers for heavier fabrics. Specialty needles take care of leather or metallic embroidery. The best thing to do if you are confused is to read the package, which usually describes what the needle is for. Universal needles, around size 10–11, are perfect for beginners, but if you're venturing out into new fabric realms, try to find a needle that matches your selection the best.

Hand-sewing needles: There are specific needles for hand sewing, and these are called "sharps." They come in a range of sizes, though as the needles get larger, they are usually labeled for embroidery and tapestry sewing. Find a size that feels comfortable for you within the sharps range.

Thread: Thread is the glue that's going to hold all your projects together, so it's good to get acquainted with it. While there are quite a few different forms of thread out there, be sure to look for all-purpose thread. This is a polyester blend of thread that works wonderfully for everything. Shiny rayon threads are meant for embroidery and all cotton threads for hand quilting, which isn't what we need here for sewing home décor projects. You will want to pick a thread that matches your fabric so contrasting colors don't peek out of your project. To see if your thread matches your fabric, hold a length of the thread across the fabric and see if it blends in. If you can't find the perfect color, go with a shade darker rather than lighter.

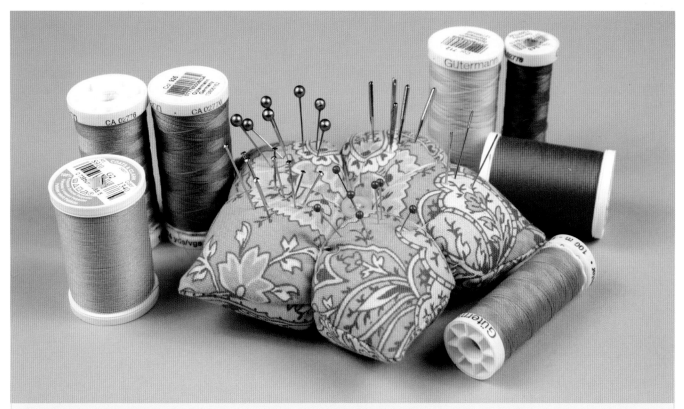

Pins, needles & thread: The glue that holds all your projects together.

Additional Supplies

In addition to basic tools and fabric, some projects call for special supplies. Some are called notions, others embellishments, but all are quite standard, easy to find, and helpful to keep around for other projects in the future.

Rotary cutter: Working much like a pizza cutter, a rotary cutter is a sharp-bladed tool that can cut long straight lines in a snap. It's a boon for quilting, and works best with a ruler to keep cuts straight and a mat underneath to protect surfaces from the sharp blade.

Pinking shears: Woven fabrics like cotton and flannel tend to unravel when their edges are left raw. A fast way of finishing those edges is with pinking shears, which cut the fabric in a zigzag pattern and prevent the edges from fraying to bits.

Ribbon: Ribbon is not only adorable for embellishment, but also has practical uses such as for closures or creating gathers. It comes in many widths and colors, so it can add a distinctive look to your project.

Bias tape: Made from cloth fabric cut on the bias (for a slight, but smooth, stretch), bias tape comes in many colors and is used to bind raw edges of fabrics quickly and easily. When the folded fabric is opened, it fits snugly over the raw edge and is sewn down.

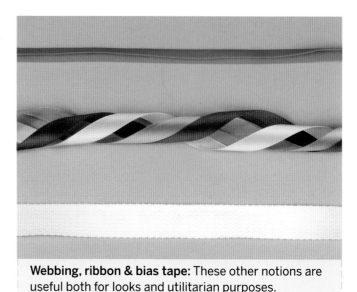

Webbing, ribbon & bias tape: These other notions are useful both for looks and utilitarian purposes.

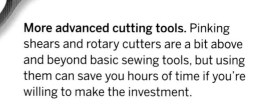

More advanced cutting tools. Pinking shears and rotary cutters are a bit above and beyond basic sewing tools, but using them can save you hours of time if you're willing to make the investment.

Hook-and-loop tape: Hook-and-loop tape is a simple kind of closure that's great for beginners because it doesn't require any fiddling with buttons, zippers, or snaps. Go with the sew-on variety to make sure it stays in place.

Elastic: Standard elastic can be used to create gathers in fabric or cinch in roomy pockets. The more decorative varieties can be used on the outside of projects like wearables to add a unique touch.

Batting: Polyester batting is a definite go-to filling for plush items like pillows. You can also choose from the other fillings, such as micro pellets.

Quilt batting: This long and thin sheet of batting is made specifically for quilts. The polyester varieties are much fluffier, while the cotton varieties are thinner and denser. They typically come in packages for a specific blanket size or by the yard.

Beeswax: While not absolutely necessary for most projects, beeswax is useful for adding strength to thread for hand sewing. Running thread along a beeswax block coats it and prevents breaking and knots. The real advantage of strengthening the thread is to create long-lasting seams for your projects.

Varieties of elastic: Strong (but plain) bands of elastic are primarily used for their tough and stretchy qualities, while lacey decorative elastic is more delicate and cannot stand up to as much pulling.

Interfacing: This material is used for stabilizing and giving greater support to fabric. It comes in iron- and sew-on varieties, as well as various weights. When attached to your fabric, it will make the fabric more stable and rigid. This is perfect if you want to use a lightweight fabric for a project that would normally require a heavyweight fabric, or to eliminate any stretching that your fabric might have. Interfacing also helps your projects keep their shape when you want them to have a particular look. Interfacing is sold by the yard or in precut packages. The majority of interfacing comes in 22" (56cm)-wide widths, so the projects in this book will reflect that when listing required materials.

Fusible fleece: Similar to interfacing is fusible fleece. It is a fiber that adheres to your fabric, just like interfacing, but provides cushion as well as support. Your fabric will be rigid and keep its shape, but also be slightly padded. In addition, there are also insulated varieties. Fusible fleece also comes by the yard or in precut packages. Most fusible and insulated fleece comes in 22" (56cm)-wide widths, so the projects in this book will reflect that when listing required materials.

Fusible web: Used in this book for appliqué, fusible web is a paper-backed adhesive that is adhered to your selected fabric with an iron. After peeling the paper away, the adhesive is left behind and can then be ironed to another surface. The lightweight variety is for appliqué that will be stitched, while the heavyweight variety is for embellishments that aren't meant to be sewn, making it better for projects that won't get a lot of wear and tear. Fusible web is sold by the yard and in packages. See how fusible web is used in the appliqué feature (page 39).

Stabilizer: Stabilizer is often used in tandem with fusible web for the appliqué process. The dense stitches used for appliqué can often warp or put strain on fabric. Stabilizer prevents that from happening. Light- to medium-weight stabilizer is best for these projects, because the leftover margins can be torn away after use.

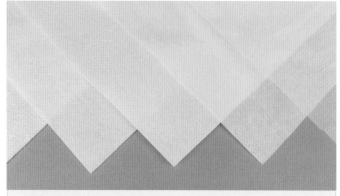

Interfacing & fusible fleece: Interfacing adds stability to fabrics and comes in light-, medium-, and heavyweight varieties. Other special interfacings are fusible fleece and insulated fleece.

Sewing Techniques and Terms

Phrases and terms such as these might pop up in the directions for your project, and if you don't know what they mean, this is a good place to start to get the jargon cleared up.

MACHINE STITCHES

Basic stitch:
Width: 0
Length: Short to medium
This stitch is ideal for all of your general seaming needs. Go shorter for lighter, more delicate fabrics, and a bit longer for thicker, sturdier fabrics.

Basting and gathering stitch:
Width: 0
Length: Long
A straight stitch at maximum length is used for basting. This is a seam that's meant to hold fabric temporarily in place where it can't be seen or will be removed later. This is also used for gathering fabric to make items like ruffles. Learn more about that on page 35.

Buttonhole stitch:
Width: Narrow
Length: Short
A narrow and short zigzag stitch is what's used when making a buttonhole. Most machines come equipped with a feature to do this automatically, but if yours doesn't, it can be made freehand with this stitch.

Stretch stitch:
Width: Narrow
Length: Medium to long
A narrow zigzag with a longer length is used as a basic stretch stitch. When sewing knit fabrics, your finished seams will stretch along with the fabric when sewn with these stitches.

Appliqué zigzag stitch:
Width: Medium to wide
Length: Short
A medium to wide zigzag done in a short length makes a great stitch for sewing appliqué fabric. Turn to the appliqué feature (page 39) to see it in action.

Finishing stitch:
Width: Medium
Length: Medium to long
A basic zigzag stitch is perfect for finishing the edges of your fabric so they don't unravel. This can be done within the seam allowance or over the edge of the fabric.

Couching stitch:
Width: Wide
Length: Medium to long
Couching is a kind of decorative technique that sews down cords, yarn, or other embellishments to your fabric. This same technique can sew down a thin piece of ribbon or string that can be used to easily gather your fabric.

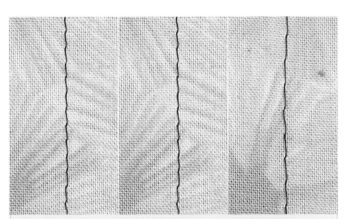

Straight stitches: Vary your stitch length to get short stitches suitable for fine fabrics, medium length stitches for light- to medium-weight fabrics, and long stitches for basting and gathering.

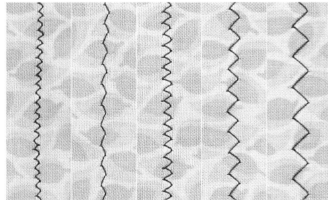

Zigzag stitches: Vary your stitch length and width to get stitches for buttonholes, knit fabrics, appliqué, finishing, and couching.

HAND SEWING

Just a bit of hand sewing practice can get you through the projects in this book. Here are the stitches that come up most frequently.

Make a knot at the tail ends of your thread, or make a knot in your fabric before you start stitching. Do this by weaving the needle through a small bit of fabric, around ⅛" (0.5cm), and then pull the thread until the tail ends stick out by about 1" (2.5cm). Repeat the same stitch in the same spot, but before you tighten the stitch, loop the needle through the loop in your thread similar to a half-hitch knot.

Backstitch: This is the basic hand-sewing stitch used in place of a sewing machine stitch. After creating your knot in the thread or fabric, insert your needle into the beginning of the seam. Bring it up about ½" (1.5cm) away. Insert the needle again, going backward about ¼" (0.5cm), and then up ¼" (0.5cm) beyond the previous stitch. This is a constant "two steps forward, one step back" rhythm that creates a very neat, yet strong, seam.

Basting stitch: This is a simple hand-sewing stitch that replaces the basting stitches done by your machine. You'll have much more control and can hold your fabric together without the aid of sharp pins! If you plan to remove these stitches later, avoid making a knot in your thread or fabric. Instead leave a very long thread tail to keep your seam from unraveling. Insert your needle into the beginning of the seam, and weave it back and forth through the layers by about 1" (2.5cm) per stitch.

Ladder stitch: This stitch is also known as a slip stitch, because you are slipping the needle into the folds of fabric to bring two folded edges together. This results in a nearly invisible seam that can be done from the outside of your project.

Create a knot from the inside of your project so it doesn't show, and then begin by weaving the needle in and out of one fold in your fabric, making a stitch about ¼" (0.5cm) long. Move to the next side, progressing forward, and repeat the same stitch. Tighten the stitches lightly as you go along, and you'll see the ladder shape formed by the threads will disappear into the fabric.

Create a knot at the end in the fabric, and then insert the needle beside the knot and through the project, pulling it away from your seam. Clip the thread while you pull and the thread tail will disappear into the finished project.

Knot your thread. Instead of creating a knot at the end of your thread, it's much more secure to create one tied into the fabric itself.

Backstitch: If you need to hand sew a seam that replaces a sewing machine stitch, the backstitch is the way to go.

Basting stitch: This stitch works well for temporary seams or for making ruffles as described on page 35.

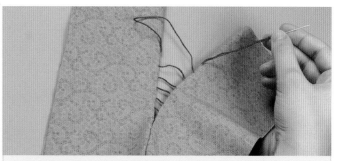

Ladder stitch: Also known as a slip stitch, this creates a nearly invisible seam from the outside of your project.

ADDITIONAL TERMS

Pattern symbols and guidelines: Pattern guidelines and symbols may differ, so it always helps to read over patterns and instructions before jumping into a project. The patterns from this book will list seam allowances, fold lines, seam lines, and grain lines. The circle symbols indicate where seams break and an opening is left, and gray lines show where to place appliqué or other project pieces. Mark these on your fabric using tracing paper or a fabric marker. The patterns will also indicate how many of each piece to cut, and in what color and fabric if it's helpful for the look of the project.

Seam allowance: This is the space between the edge of your fabric and where the seam is made. The standard for most U.S. patterns is ⅝" (1.5cm), though it can vary depending on the project and how small it is. Always check the pattern to know what your seam allowance is.

Grain line: The grain line of a fabric follows the direction in which the fabric was knitted or woven and goes parallel to the selvedge (the machine finished edges of the fabric). The pattern pieces have a grain line arrow that indicates how the pattern piece should be placed to ensure proper stretching and drape in the right directions.

Finishing edges: The raw edges of woven fabrics tend to unravel and fray apart if left unfinished. If you are using woven fabrics in your project, any exposed edges should be finished. This can be done with pinking shears, a zigzag stitch within the seam allowance, or with fray-blocking liquid.

Finishing edges. Certain fabrics can sometimes unravel when worked with or washed. Prevent this with pinking shears, a zigzag stitch, or fray-blocking liquid.

Clipping corners and curves: When sewing pieces that will be turned right-side out, the seam allowances of convex corners and curves should be clipped or trimmed to accommodate excess fabric when the shape is inverted. Alternately, the seam allowances of concave corners and curves should be clipped or trimmed to accommodate the fabric stretching when the shape is inverted.

Box stitch: This is done around the ends of straps or tabs attached to a project for added support and strength. They are done by sewing a square around the end of the strap and then going diagonally across the square, creating an hourglass shape within the square. A single square without the X can be done for ease, but the X gives the greatest hold. Be sure to do lots of backstitching at the beginning and end of this seam for the greatest strength.

Topstitching: This is done for decorative and strength-increasing purposes for the outside of a project. Choose a thread that you are fine with being visible, and sew another seam about ¼" (0.5cm) from the previous seam. This creates a professional touch.

Clipping corners and curves. Seam allowances of curves and corners should be clipped before turning the pieces right side out.

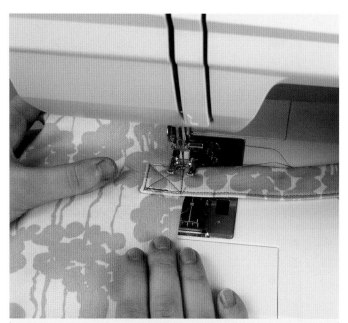

Box stitch. A box stitch is the go-to stitch for creating the most strength in a small space, so it's ideal for straps, hangers, and the like.

Hems: Single- and double-fold hems are the type of hems used for the projects in this book. These types of hems are done by folding the fabric by the measurement indicated in the directions either once or twice and ironing to make a firm crease. Sew the fold down and the hem is complete. A double-fold hem finishes a raw edge.

Darts: Darts are triangle-shaped tucks made in the fabric to create a pronounced, three-dimensional shape in the fabric piece. These are made by folding the triangle mark in half and sewing along one edge of the triangle. If the dart is big enough, cut it open and press the halves outward. If not, press it to one side.

Gathering: Ruffles or gathers are made in fabric by sewing two lines of very long straight stitches (without backstitching) within the seam allowance of your fabric piece. Tie the threads at one end of the fabric and pull on the bobbin threads at the other end. Once the piece is gathered to the desired size, knot the bobbin threads and machine sew the edge to hold the gathers in place.

Darts. Darts create a three-dimensional shape in otherwise two-dimensional fabric.

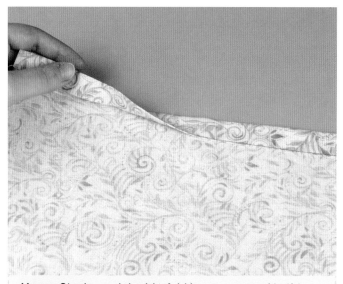

Hems. Single- and double-fold hems are used in this book for unfinished edges.

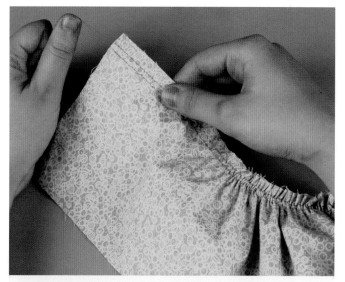

Gathers. When you pull at the bobbin threads of a seam with very long stitches, ruffles are made in the fabric.

Sewing Knit Fabrics

Once you've gotten a handle on sewing with different weights and textures of woven fabrics, why not try out knits? They can be a little unpredictable at times, and that's why it helps to have some background knowledge about fabrics so you can be ready for anything unexpected the knits might throw at you.

Varieties of knits: As mentioned in the fabrics section (page 14), there are large varieties of light- and medium-weight knits to choose from. Medium-weight knits typically stretch less than lightweight knits and are therefore easier to sew. Start with the thicker varieties before working your way down to slinkier fabrics.

Knit grain lines: It's very important to keep to your grain line when working with knits. Because knits stretch across the horizontal grain (and sometimes also the vertical grain), it's crucial that the pattern pieces line up to go along with this stretch. A t-shirt wouldn't fit as well if it only stretched up and down and didn't stretch around your body, would it? So think one step ahead if you can and imagine where the fabric needs to stretch when you cut it.

Cutting knits: Some lightweight knits can be slinky and move in unpredictable ways while you cut them. A good way to tame these fabrics is to lay them on tissue paper (or newspaper if you don't mind washing off ink) before you cut them. As you pin your pieces and cut them, make sure you go through all the layers. Try to downgrade to your craft scissors for this if possible, as the tissue paper can dull your sewing shears.

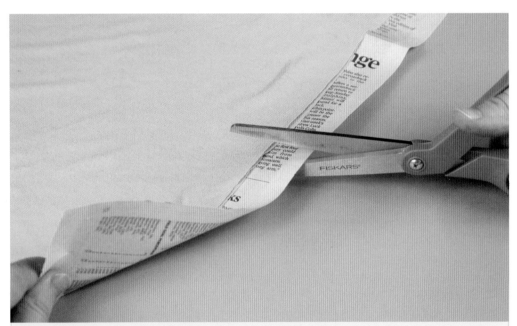

Cutting knits: Cut your knit fabrics with a layer of tissue or newspaper underneath for more stability, but be sure to use craft scissors if you can.

Sewing needle for knits: There are special sewing machine needles designed for knit fabrics. They have a rounded tip that allows the needle to punch between the threads rather than right through. If your seams aren't turning out how you'd like, check to be sure that you're using a sewing needle for knits.

Stretch stitches: Because your finished garment will be stretchy, your seams should stretch along with it or the threads might break. If your machine has a stretch stitch, then you're in business! It will often use a kind of two-steps-forward, one-step-back motion that works to give the garment some stretch. If your machine doesn't have a stretch stitch, a zigzag stitch with a narrow width and medium length is a great substitute.

The problem with knits: The main issue with knits is how they tend to stretch while you sew them. No matter how little you touch the fabric, the pressure of the presser foot and the pulling of the needle seem to do something that gives you warped, wavy seams—especially at the hems. However, once you finally get things working in your favor and your seams are perfectly flat and neat, knits are joy to work with! Your seams will look much more fluid and smooth, your garments will fit you comfortably and perfectly, and you don't have to worry about finished seams! Knits don't unravel, so putting together knit projects is super quick! Here are some tips for keeping your knits from stretching out of shape while you sew:

Hands off: Even if you might not realize it, you could be pushing or pulling at your fabric while you sew. Try to consciously put less pressure on the fabric while you guide it and your seams might turn out better.

Stretch stitches: A narrow zigzag stitch or machine stretch stitch will allow your seams to stretch along with your knit fabrics.

Ease the presser foot: If your machine has an adjustable presser control for the presser foot, bring it down to the lowest pressure (but not 0). The presser foot won't push down as much on the fabric, so it won't cause it to stretch.

Easing: Easing is a technique usually used for woven fabrics to give the fabric a light, even, and almost unnoticeable distribution of gathers along an edge. In knit fabrics, this works to prevent stretched stitches and puckers. While you sew your seam, press down behind the fabric so the fabric feeding through the machine begins to build up. Your sewing will start to slow down, and when it slows to almost no motion, let the fabric go and press your finger down again.

Stabilizing: If your knits are still giving you trouble, especially if they are thin enough that the needle forces them down through the throat plate, stabilizer is a very reliable solution. Use tissue paper, newspaper, or very lightweight stabilizer beneath your fabric as you sew. When you finish, gently tear the paper away from your stitches to avoid breaking them.

Ironing: Even if your stitches seem a little wobbly after you sew, try giving them an iron to see if they smooth out. In a lot of cases they will improve quite a bit, so there's no need to worry about how your seams look right out of the machine.

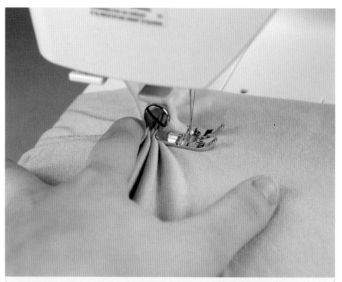

Easing: This is a subtle technique that creates light gathers in your fabric, effectively canceling out the stretching that might happen while you sew knits.

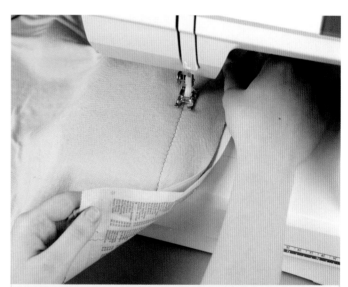

Stabilizing your stitches: As a trump card, layering tissue or newspaper beneath your fabric will stop any stretching dead in its tracks. Just be careful when tearing away the paper afterward.

Appliqué

Appliqué is one of the main embellishment techniques used in this book to decorate projects. It is the process of sewing one small shape of fabric on top of another larger piece for decorative purposes. For machine appliqué, however, there are a few different methods that can suit your skill level, resources, or desired look.

APPLIQUÉ SUPPLIES

The simplest version of appliqué can be done with fabrics that are lighter than the base fabric, such as cotton or twill. More professional-looking appliqué can be achieved by adding fusible web and stabilizer.

Fabrics: Most every kind of fabric can be appliquéd, and a good rule of thumb is to use a fabric that is lighter than the fabric you're appliquéing on. Fabrics like cotton, flannel, and felt are a good choice, but even thinner twill, home décor, and faux suede fabrics would work well. Most of these fabrics will fray if their raw edges are exposed. That could be the look you're going for, but if not, be sure to choose your appliqué method accordingly.

Fusible web: Used in this book for appliqué, fusible web is a paper-backed adhesive. When it's ironed to almost any fabric, it makes it an iron-on patch. This patch can then be adhered and sewn to your project with ease. It is nearly indispensible for small and lightweight appliqué pieces. However, it is optional for larger, thicker pieces of appliqué, which may only need some sewing pins to hold them in place. The lightweight variety of fusible web is ideal for appliqué and is sold by the yard or in precut packages.

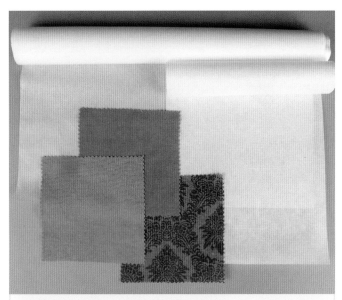

Appliqué supplies: Appliqué can easily be done using the fabric of your choice and fusible web and stabilizer for extra support.

Stabilizer: Often used in tandem with fusible web, stabilizer prevents warping and shifting of fabric during the appliqué process. It's very helpful for lightweight appliqué pieces and when using the satin stitch method, but is less necessary for more stable fabrics or when using the straight and zigzag stitch methods. Lightweight to medium-weight stabilizer suits appliqué best and can be found by the yard or in precut packages.

APPLIQUÉ TECHNIQUES

Applying one decorative fabric to another can be done in a number of different ways. You can choose which one you like depending on the difficulty or finished look you are going for. Here are some easy and surefire methods you can try:

Adhesive method:
Fusible web: Heavy-duty
Stitch: None
Fabric: Felt
This method uses only fusible web to adhere the appliqué fabric. This is a great simple method for projects that won't receive a lot of washing. After applying the fusible web to your appliqué fabric, iron it to your finished project following the manufacturer's instructions. Just like an iron-on patch, the heavy-duty adhesive will hold the fabric there indefinitely!

Floating method:
Fusible web: None
Stitch: Straight
Fabric: Felt
This is what I use to describe the appliqué method in which only a small section of the fabric is sewn down and the rest floats free for a charming three-dimensional effect. Lay your appliqué fabric onto your main fabric and sew it down with a straight stitch along the lines that the pattern indicates, typically along the center of the piece.

Straight stitch method:
Fusible web: Light
Stitch: Straight
Fabric: Felt
With this method, you stitch the edges of your appliqué fabric completely to your main fabric, but you do so easily with just a straight stitch. Use fusible web to adhere your appliqué fabric to the main fabric. Sew along the edge of the appliqué fabric, about ⅛" (0.5cm) in from the edge.

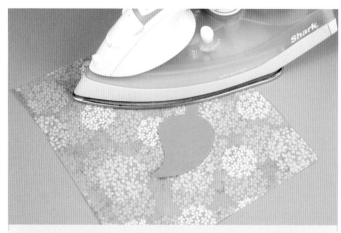

Adhesive method: With just some heavy-duty fusible web, you can iron on any felt appliqué as easily as an iron-on patch.

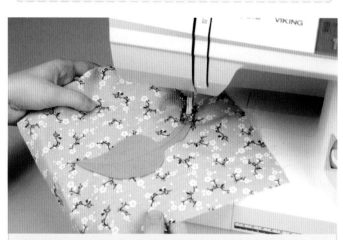

Floating method: A simple straight stitch down the middle of a felt shape is enough to hold it in place and leaves the rest free for added dimension.

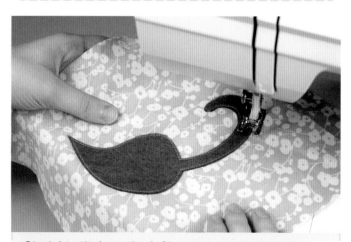

Straight stitch method: Choose a contrasting color thread for a cute shabby-chic look.

Zigzag method:

Fusible web: Light
Stitch: Zigzag
Fabric: Felt or cotton

This method takes longer than those listed on page 40, but allows you to use cotton as your appliqué fabric without fear of it unraveling. Adhere your appliqué fabric to the main fabric with fusible web. Using a zigzag stitch of short length (0.75–1.25) and medium to wide width (2–4.5), sew along the edges of the appliqué fabric, covering the raw edge of the fabric.

Satin stitch method:

Fusible web: Medium-weight
Stitch: Zigzag
Fabric: Felt or cotton

After applying the appliqué pieces, sew a medium to wide width and very short length (usually the shortest your machine can handle) zigzag stitch over the edge of the pieces. This takes more patience and coordination, but yields a very professional result. Medium-weight stabilizer is recommended, because the dense stitches can warp the main fabric.

This option completely encases the raw edges of the appliqué piece in thread, so there is no need to worry about unraveling. Complementary thread colors can also be used, and embroidery threads work especially well in this application, as the finished product has a beautiful sheen.

Zigzag method: Use a narrow width zigzag stitch for small appliqué pieces and a wider stitch for larger pieces.

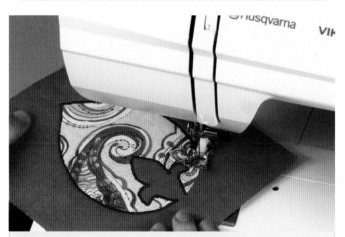

Satin stitch: This appliqué method uses a medium to wide width zigzag stitch at the shortest of lengths. The stitches are so close that no fabric from the appliqué piece peeks through and a professional-looking line of stitches is created.

Following the Projects

Now that you've refreshed yourself on the basics, it's time to dive into your first project. The projects in this book generally work from the simplest to the most time-intensive and complex, allowing you to improve your skills as you go. There will be lots of other useful sewing tips and techniques to learn along the way as well.

With each project, you'll find a tools and materials list, listing all the fabric and other supplies you'll need, as well as in what quantities. As mentioned before, fabrics come in varying widths and the materials list will state how many yards you'll need depending on the width. If the list doesn't specify, then either width is fine. The tools you need are also listed, including your basic sewing kit and any additional tools.

Although every project is suitable for beginners, you'll find that they are rated from one to eight stars based on the estimated time needed, the additional techniques used, and the overall complexity of the project.

⭐ If you've never picked up a needle, start with these! They usually require one to three very easy techniques and take mere minutes to make.

⭐⭐ Your beginner's jitters have worn off and you're not so anxious to cut into your fabric anymore. These projects require one to three simple techniques or take about an hour to make.

⭐⭐⭐ You're starting to understand the basic principles and are eager to see how they work together. These projects require two to four simple techniques or take a little more than an hour or so to make.

⭐⭐⭐⭐ You've had a few ah-ha! moments and new techniques sound exciting rather than scary to you. These projects may have one or two intermediate techniques or take between one and two hours to make.

⭐⭐⭐⭐⭐ Using your machine has started to become natural, and you barely have to look at your manual or cheat sheet anymore. These projects may have two or three intermediate techniques or take two hours or so to make.

⭐⭐⭐⭐⭐⭐ Using techniques now feels completely natural and you barely have to check up on how to do them anymore. These projects may have three or four intermediate techniques or take between two and three hours to make.

⭐⭐⭐⭐⭐⭐⭐ The mechanics of sewing and assembling fabric pieces now start to make sense, and you can see where your project is going as you assemble it. These projects may have one or two advanced techniques or take about an afternoon of work to make.

⭐⭐⭐⭐⭐⭐⭐⭐ You feel like you're really in the zone and you're ready to take on anything! These projects have three or four advanced techniques or take a few afternoons of work to make.

USING THE PATTERNS

Each project comes with pattern pieces either printed in the book with the project or listed as squares that you should cut. The printed patterns can be enlarged at a copy center or on your personal computer so they can be cut out with craft scissors.

The printed patterns list everything you need to know so you can work with them in the easiest way possible, including the pattern piece name, the seam allowance, the seam line, the number you should cut, and what fabric and color you should cut it from if applicable.

Each pattern also has a grain line, which indicates in what direction the pattern should be placed when it's cut from the fabric.

For square patterns, the project will list dimensions you can use to cut the pieces straight from your fabric without requiring a pattern piece. However, because it's always smarter to measure twice and cut once, I sometimes like to measure these pattern pieces from newspaper and use those on the fabric rather than cutting straight from the material.

Stars to Caffeine!

Ranking these projects with stars is very straightforward and easy to follow—perfect if you're just starting out. I must confess that I'm a bit of a foodie, though, so I often think of the level of difficulty of each project in terms of food. For example: sourness! In this case, the easiest projects might be called tangerines, and the hardest projects grapefruits. Or spiciness, where the easiest projects are green peppers and the hardest are ghost peppers! One of my favorite ways to think about project difficulty is by level of caffeine. Easier projects are perfect for working during a lazy afternoon and sipping your favorite cup of green tea, while for the harder ones, you might need to break out the espresso! If I were to translate these projects to level of caffeine, this is what they would look like:

| White Tea | Green Tea | Black Tea | Cappuccino | Latte | Cuppa' Joe | French Roast | Espresso |

If you were to choose a way to represent a project's difficulty level, how would you do it?

PREPARING YOUR FABRIC

When you have your fabrics ready for your project, you should first be sure to prewash them if they're brand new. Fabric bolts at the store list the washing instructions, though basic beginner fabrics rarely require special washing processes. Prewashing eliminates the light starch that tends to be applied to retail fabrics, and it also gets any shrinkage out of the way.

If your fabric is wrinkle-prone, be sure to iron it smooth before cutting from it. The most typical way to cut pattern pieces is to fold the fabric in half so the selvedge edges meet. The selvedge edges are the machine-finished edges of your fabric; you'll notice that they're a lot stiffer than the rest of the fabric. Check to see if your fabric has a direction to it. If the prints or designs all point in one direction, you'll want your pattern pieces aligned so the pattern matches. It's a persnickety thing, so it's only really important with big graphics. You'd hate to have your new shower curtain covered with upside-down fish! To assist with this, the grain lines on each pattern piece indicate the direction the design should point in. For the best results, make sure the grain line is parallel to the selvedge edge of your fabric.

Next, you'll want to pin your pattern pieces to your fabric exactly the same way as pinning fabric together. Weave the pins in then out of the layers of fabric and paper. Pin down all your pattern pieces at once, trying to leave as little space between them as possible to get the most out of your fabric. Because you're cutting your fabric on a folded sheet, notice that you'll get two pieces at once. This is not only a time saver, but it's typical practice in sewing, as most projects are designed to be symmetrical. Your pattern will indicate how many pieces you need to cut. It's usually two, but if not, unfold your fabric before cutting.

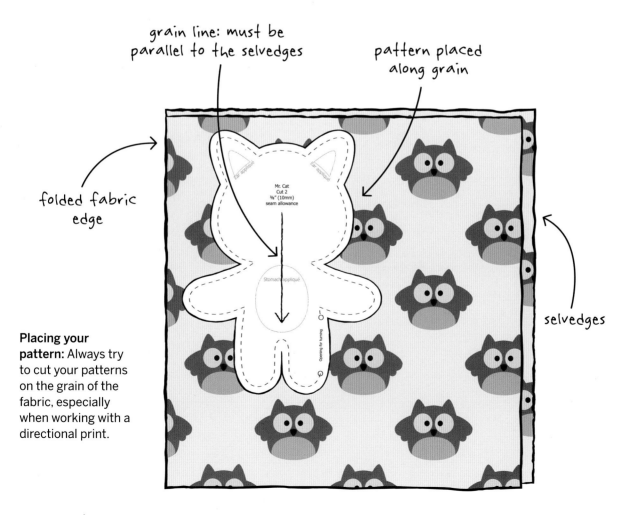

grain line: must be parallel to the selvedges

pattern placed along grain

folded fabric edge

selvedges

Mr. Cat
Cut 2
⅜" (10mm)
seam allowance

Placing your pattern: Always try to cut your patterns on the grain of the fabric, especially when working with a directional print.

CUTTING YOUR PATTERN PIECES

Once you have all your pattern pieces pinned, it's time to cut them out. Cut as closely as possible to the outside edge of your patterns. If your scissors are sharp, you shouldn't have any issue getting clean and smooth cuts.

When all your pieces are cut from the fabric, begin to remove your patterns. Using your fabric marker, transfer any markings from the patterns to the fabric. Check the project page for any additional markings that need to be made. Another helpful trick is to label your pattern pieces. If you have adhesive labels on hand, those are perfect, but masking tape works well in a pinch. Label the right side of the fabric, and write the name of the pattern piece so you'll know when to use it. Now you'll always know what side is the right side and make sure to match it up!

All of this prep work may seem tedious, but you can take it from me that it's well worth the extra time and saves headaches and confusion in the long run. Often this start-up work takes up about half the time I spend on a project (don't worry, this time is reflected in the project time estimates!), so once you finish you can feel like you're nearly halfway there!

Label & mark your pieces: Transfer all the markings and notes from the pattern to your fabric and it will be a huge help as you embark on your project.

sew me!
Home Décor
Projects

Now that you've given yourself a refresher course
on the techniques you'll need to use, you are ready to
get sewing! Use the projects in this chapter to jazz up
your kitchen, organize your home office, or infuse your
bedroom with your personal style. Use each project as
an opportunity to express yourself, whether it's through
your fabric selection or the appliqué designs you chose
to use. If you don't love it, don't sew it!

48 Creative Coasters

52 Homey Hanging Organizer

58 Reversible Duvet Cover

65 Cute Cube Storage Boxes

70 Ruffled Pillow Cover

78 Modernist Quilt

88 Curtains for Window or Shower

Creative Coasters

★ ☆ ☆ ☆ ☆ ☆ ☆ ☆

🕐 **ESTIMATED TIME:**
20–40 minutes

⊐ **TECHNIQUES:**
Sewing Curves,
Appliqué, Hemming

✓ **MAKES:**
One 4" (10cm)-diameter coaster

These super simple coasters are a perfect quick addition to your home. Practice sewing curves and add an appliqué fleur-de-lys, pomegranate, or daisy for fun!

Materials

☐ Fat quarter of quilting cotton or 6" x 15" (15 x 30.5cm) scrap of light-to medium-weight woven fabric

☐ 6" x 6" (15 x 15cm) square of scrap felt

☐ Fat quarter or 6" x 6" (15 x 15cm) scrap of appliqué fabric (optional)

☐ 6" x 6" (15 x 15cm) square of fusible web (optional)

Tools

☐ Basic sewing kit (see page 25)

Your collection of fabric pieces for this project should look something like this:

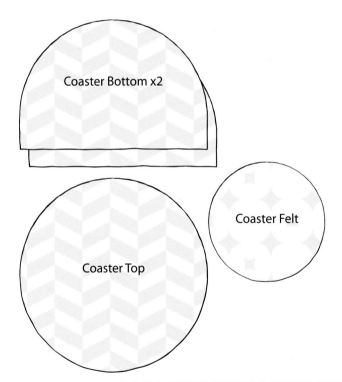

THE PREP WORK:
Cut your fabric pieces using the patterns on page 51. Copy any markings from the patterns.

Creative Coasters (continued)

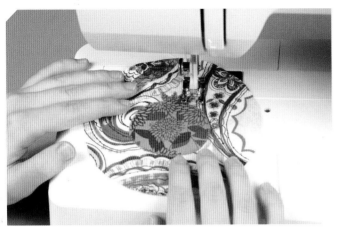

1 **Appliqué your design (optional).** See the Getting Started chapter (page 39) to choose a method for applying your decorative fabric to your coaster top. Sew your appliqué in the center of the coaster top, or at least 1" (2.5cm) in from the edge of the fabric.

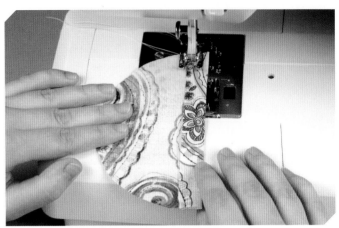

2 **Hem the bottom pieces.** Fold over ⅝" (1.5cm) along the top straight edge of the coaster bottom pieces toward the wrong side. Sew this fold in place close to the raw edge to create a single-fold hem for each piece.

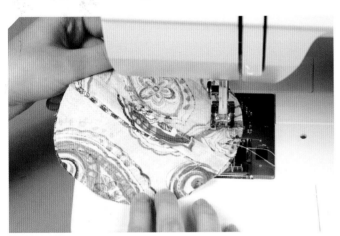

3 **Sew the perimeter.** Layer the bottom pieces over the top with right sides together. Line the edges up, and the bottom pieces should overlap in the middle. Sew entirely around the perimeter of the coaster.

4 **Add the bottom.** Notch the curves, turn the coaster right side out from the middle opening, and press flat. Center the middle felt piece over the bottom and sew it to the coaster around the edge.

Experiment!

Get yourself a machine needle for vinyl and use laminated media (page 24) or fused plastic (page 22) to create recycled coasters. Be sure to cut two of the Coaster Top and skip the Coaster Bottom. Sew the circles together as described in Step 3 with wrong sides together, and don't worry about hemming or turning right side out! Or, try using terry cloth for one or both sides of the coaster. They'll absorb all those little spills and look adorable as well!

Creative Coasters Patterns

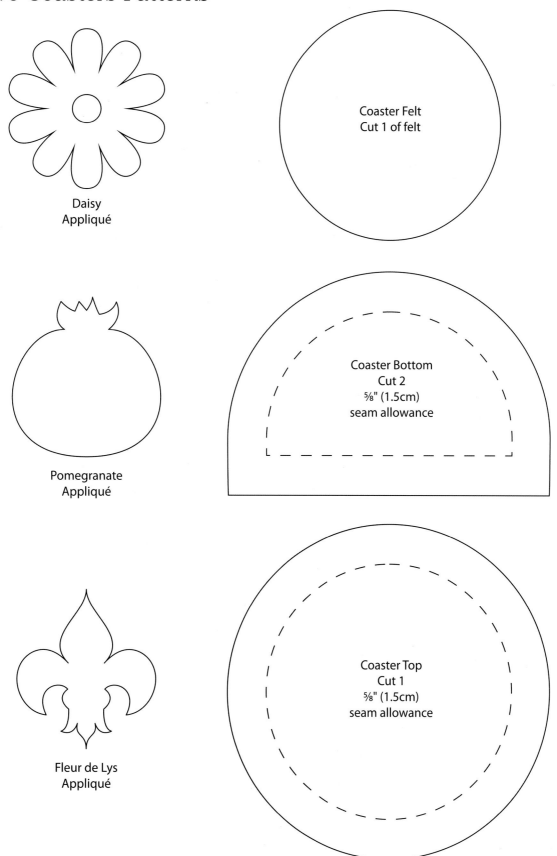

Daisy
Appliqué

Coaster Felt
Cut 1 of felt

Pomegranate
Appliqué

Coaster Bottom
Cut 2
⅝" (1.5cm)
seam allowance

Fleur de Lys
Appliqué

Coaster Top
Cut 1
⅝" (1.5cm)
seam allowance

Enlarge patterns 150% for actual size.

Homey Hanging Organizer

★ ★ ★ ☆ ☆ ☆ ☆ ☆

ESTIMATED TIME:
1 hour

TECHNIQUES:
Appliqué

MAKES:
One 7" x 21" (17.5 x 53.5cm) organizer

This project takes a little more investment, but is definitely worth the extra time! Use the loop at the top to hang it off a key hook, bathroom hook, or anywhere else to hold extra little necessities. It's great for organizing mail or stashing toiletries. The additional gourd and teapot appliqué pieces are an adorable feature, but the alphabet appliqué patterns are truly special, and can be used for monogramming your pockets!

Materials

- ☐ ½ yd. (50cm) of medium- to heavyweight woven fabric
- ☐ Fat quarter or 12" x 12" (30.5 x 30.5cm) scrap of appliqué fabric (optional)
- ☐ 12" x 12" (30.5 x 30.5cm) square of fusible web (optional)

Tools

- ☐ Basic sewing kit (see page 25)
- ☐ Safety pin
- ☐ Chopstick or similar turning tool

Your collection of fabric pieces for this project should look something like this:

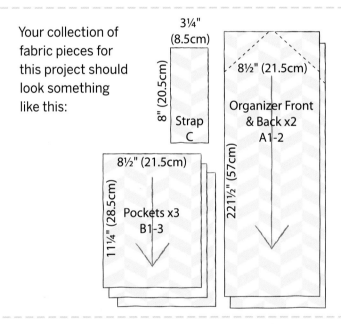

THE PREP WORK:

Cut your fabric pieces from the following chart. Cut any additional appliqué pieces from the patterns on pages 56–57.

Hanging Organizer Pieces

Piece Name	Material to Cut	Size to Cut	Number to Cut	Seam Allowance
Organizer Front & Back (A1–2)	Medium-weight woven	8½" x 22½"(21.5 x 57cm)	2	⅝" (1.5cm)
Pockets (B1-3)	Medium-weight woven	8½" x 11¼"(21.5 x 28.5cm)	3	⅝" (1.5cm)
Strap (C)	Medium-weight woven	3¼" x 8"(8.5 x 20.5cm)	1	⅝" (1.5cm)
Appliqué design (optional)	Appliqué fabric and fusible web	To fit design	1	None

Homey Hanging Organizer (continued)

1 **Appliqué your design (optional).** See the Getting Started chapter to choose a method for applying your decorative fabric to the bottom of each pocket (B1–3). Center your appliqué on the pocket at least 1" (2.5cm) up from the bottom edge.

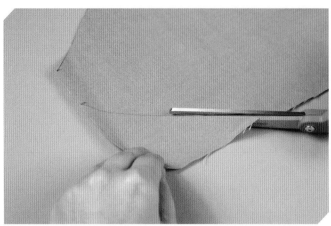

2 **Prepare the organizer front & back.** Trim the organizer front and back pieces (A1–2) to the correct shape by making a mark along the top that is 3½" (9cm) in from the left side. Measure and mark 4" (10cm) down from the top left corner. Draw a line between these points. Cut along this line to trim the triangle shape away. Repeat with the right side.

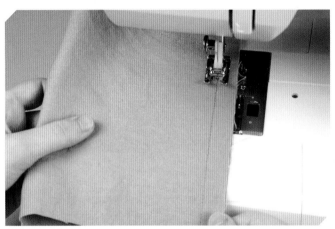

3 **Prepare the pockets.** Fold the uppermost pockets (B1–2) in half widthwise, with right sides together, and sew along the bottom raw edges. Turn them right side out and press. Mark a horizontal line 6⅝" (17cm) and 12⅝" (32cm) from the bottom of the organizer front (A1) going all the way across. This is where your uppermost pockets (B1–2) will be placed.

4 **Apply the pockets.** With the right side up, line up the bottom edge of one pocket (B1) with one of the drawn lines on right side of the organizer front (A1). Place the folded edge of the pocket so it points toward the top point of the organizer. Sew close to the bottom edge of the pocket, also known as edge stitching. Repeat this with the other pocket (B2) and the remaining drawn line.

Experiment!

When you've had some practice, try making this out of terry cloth for a perfect bathroom caddy. The absorbent fabric makes it ideal for storing toiletries that might need some time to dry after use.

Homey Hanging Organizer (continued)

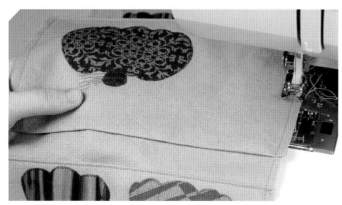

5 **Baste the pocket sides.** Fold the remaining pocket piece (B3) in half widthwise with wrong sides together and line it up along the bottom edge of the organizer front. Pin all the pockets in place along the sides. Baste all the pockets by sewing within the seam allowances along the sides and bottom of the organizer front (A1).

6 **Sew the strap.** Fold the strap (C) in half lengthwise with right sides together and sew along the open long edge, creating a tube. Turn the tube right side out and press the strap flat. You can use a safety pin to help with turning by attaching it to one end if the tube and feeding it through the tube to turn the fabric.

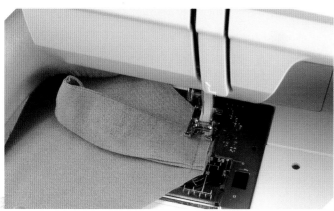

7 **Baste the strap.** Match up the short ends of the strap (C) to make a loop and baste the ends onto the pointed top of the right side of the organizer front (A1). Make sure the strap is pointing down toward the bottom of the project.

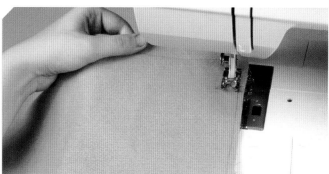

8 **Sew the front to the back.** Mark a 5" (12.5cm) line on the wrong side of the organizer back (A2), centering it along the bottom edge. This marks your opening for turning. With right sides facing, layer the front and back pieces together with the strap (C) in between them, matching up the edges. Pin all the layers together and sew along the edges, skipping the section marked along the bottom.

9 **Sew the opening closed.** Clip the seam allowances at the corners and turn your organizer right side out. Iron the organizer flat. Fold in the seam allowances around the opening in the bottom and edge stitch around the perimeter of the organizer; this should close the opening.

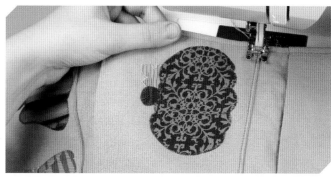

10 **Tack down the pockets.** Sew along the bottom seam of the uppermost pockets (B1–2) through all the layers. Try to sew over the previous seam for the most professional look.

Homey Hanging Organizer Patterns

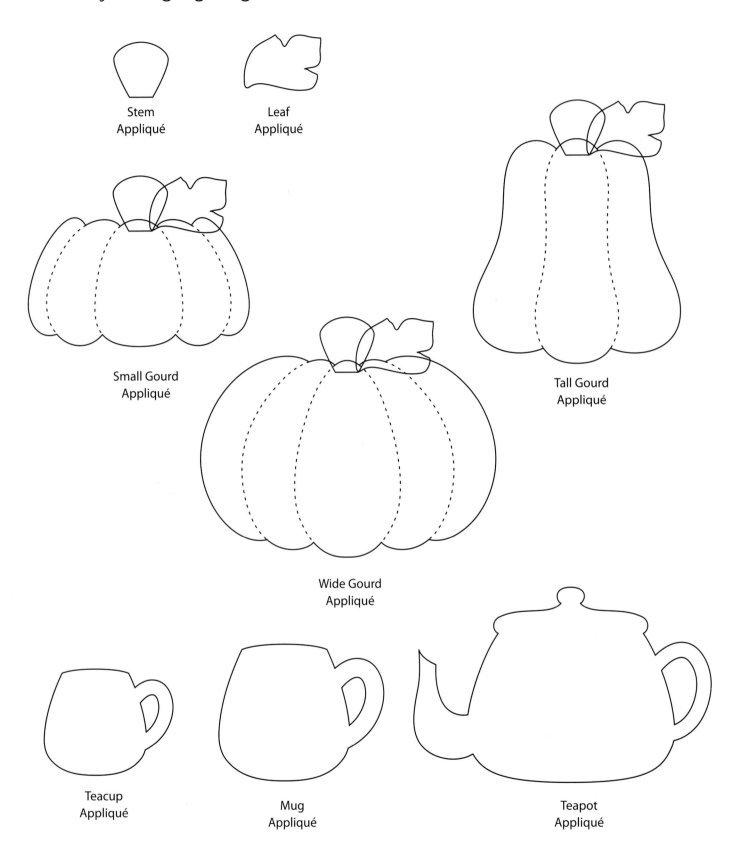

Stem
Appliqué

Leaf
Appliqué

Small Gourd
Appliqué

Tall Gourd
Appliqué

Wide Gourd
Appliqué

Teacup
Appliqué

Mug
Appliqué

Teapot
Appliqué

Enlarge patterns 125% for actual size.

Homey Hanging Organizer Patterns

Alphabet Appliqué
for Monograms

Enlarge pattern 230% for actual size.

Reversible Duvet Cover

★★★★★★★☆

⊘ **ESTIMATED TIME:**
2 hours

▣ **TECHNIQUES:**
Appliqué, Finishing Seams,
Drawstrings, Measuring

✓ **MAKES:**
One cover sized to match
your duvet

Materials

*The fabric requirements can differ
greatly depending on the size of your
duvet. Check your measurements first
if you are unsure, but here are some
rough estimates for ease:*

For king size:
☐ 8¾ yd. (875cm) quilting cotton
for back
☐ 8¾ yd. (875cm) quilting cotton
for front

For queen size:
☐ 8 yd. (800cm) quilting cotton
for front
☐ 8 yd. (800cm) quilting cotton
for back

For full/twin size:
☐ 5¼ yd. (525cm) quilting cotton
for front
☐ 5¼ yd. (525cm) quilting cotton
for back

For all sizes:
☐ Fat quarter of appliqué fabric
(optional)
☐ 1 yd. (100cm) fusible web
(optional)

Tools

☐ Basic sewing kit (see page 25)
☐ Chopstick or similar turning tool

If you've ever wanted to decorate your living space
with your own splashes of color, this is definitely
where to start! This project takes a bit of time and fabric
investment, but you'll find the techniques are really quite
easy and straightforward. With the right fabric choices,
you can make this duvet reversible, so you can flip it over
to suit whatever mood you're in. Add the Chinese symbol
or ginkgo leaf appliqué and you can change the look of
your whole room!

MEASUREMENTS

Work out these equations to find out what size pieces to cut:

Duvet width + 2½" (6.5cm) = _____ A (Cover width)

Duvet length + 3½" (9cm) = _____ B (Cover length)

Quilting cotton width – selvedges (cut them off) = _____ C
(Center panel width)

Follow these steps to find measurement D:

Take C and subtract 1¼" (3cm) = _____

Take A and subtract your solution above from it = _____

Take this new number and divide it by 2 = _____

Take this new number and add 1¼" (3cm) to it = _____ D
(side panel width)

Measure the length and width of your duvet
to determine the dimensions of your cover.

Important
The equations here
only work up to a
125" (317.5cm)-wide duvet.

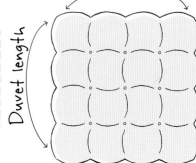

Duvet width

Duvet length

Reversible Duvet Cover *(continued)*

Your collection of fabric pieces for this project should look something like this:

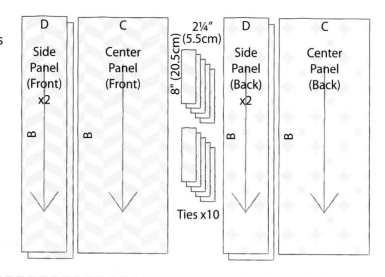

THE PREP WORK:

Using your new measurements, cut your fabric pieces following this chart.
Cut any additional appliqué pieces you desire from the patterns on pages 63–64.

Duvet Cover Pieces

Piece Name	Material to Cut	Size to Cut	Number to Cut	Seam Allowance
Center Panel (Front)	Quilting cotton for front	C x B	1	⅝" (1.5cm)
Side Panels (Front)	Quilting cotton for front	D x B	2	⅝" (1.5cm)
Center Panel (Back)	Quilting cotton for back	C x B	1	⅝" (1.5cm)
Side Panels (Back)	Quilting cotton for back	D x B	2	⅝" (1.5cm)
Ties	Coordinating quilting cotton	2¼" x 8"(5.5 x 20.5cm)	10	⅝" (1.5cm)
Appliqué design (optional)	Appliqué fabric and fusible web	To fit design	1	None

Find your style!

Skip all the hassle of buying loads of fabric and search for some second-hand bed sheets at your local thrift store. You don't even have to let sheets that are discolored with age hold you back—dye them your favorite color and you're good to go! Just be sure to find sheets that are as large as the measurements you took: A x B.

Pro tip!

It's almost impossible to cut perfectly straight lines in such long lengths, so do what the pros do. Rip your fabric! It sounds crazy, but if you notch a fabric like cotton slightly at one end, you can rip it the rest of the way in a perfectly straight line. This works best with lightweight fabrics, and might be difficult with satin and heavier fabrics. However, it's perfect for this project!

Rip it good! Thin, natural fabrics like cotton rip perfectly in a straight line along their grain!

Reversible Duvet Cover *(continued)*

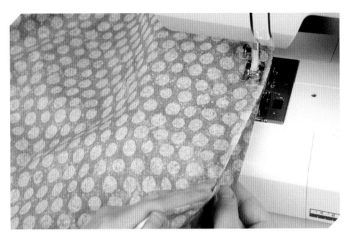

1 **Assemble the front and back.** Sew the front side panels to the front center panel along the long edges. Sew one side panel to each side of the center panel with right sides facing. Repeat this with the back side panels and back center panel.

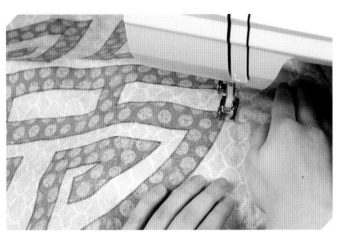

2 **Appliqué your design (optional).** See the Getting Started chapter (page 39) to choose a method for applying your decorative fabric to the front of your cover. Lay the cover front on the floor or on a large table so you can place the design properly, or fold the cover into quarters to find the exact center. Then, sew the appliqué fabric in place.

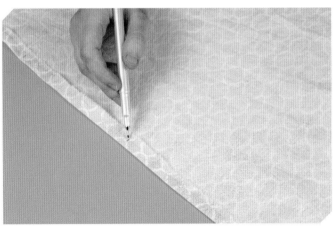

3 **Prepare the bottom edge.** Fold under the bottom edge of the front and back pieces toward the wrong side by ⅝" (1.5cm). On the wrong side of the fabric for both the front and back pieces, mark a 1 yd. (100cm)-long line centered along the bottom edge. Within this, make a mark every 6" (16.5cm). You should have five marks when finished. This is the opening where your ties will be sewn.

4 **Sew the ties.** Fold each tie piece in half lengthwise with right sides together and sew along the open long edge and one short edge. Trim the seam allowances and poke the sewn end with a chopstick to turn it right side out.

Experiment!

Is your ideal cuddle fabric a cozy t-shirt? Once you've had some experience sewing with knits, try this project out with jersey or interlock cotton! Try not to get overwhelmed by the large fabric pieces, and be sure to use all the techniques for sewing knits at your disposal if you run into trouble. In the end, you'll have one comfy duvet!

Reversible Duvet Cover *(continued)*

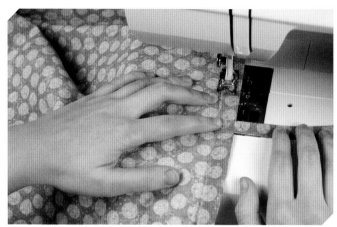

5 **Baste the ties.** Baste the raw edge of each tie to the wrong side of the bottom edge of the cover front and back. Place one tie along each marking made within the 1 yd. (100cm)-long line. Point the ties away from the cover. The front and back of the cover should each have five ties basted along the bottom edge when you are finished.

6 **Sew the bottom seam.** With right sides facing, line up the bottom edges of the cover front and back pieces and sew along the edge, skipping over the 1 yd. (100cm)-long line you marked earlier.

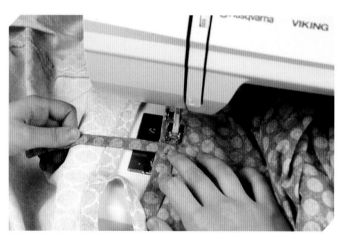

7 **Finish the bottom.** Iron the seam open and sew down the seam allowances around the opening, close to the folded edge. Avoid getting the ties caught up in the sewing. After this, fold each tie back toward the opening in the bottom and sew them in place close to the bottom edge.

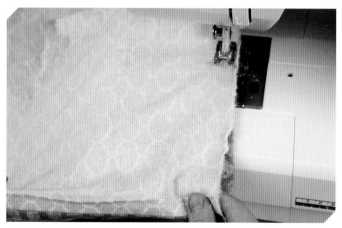

8 **Sew the sides and top.** Fold the cover along the bottom seam and match up the remaining top and side edges with right sides facing. Make sure you tuck your ties inside the cover before sewing the edges. Sew around the entire perimeter of the cover. Iron and finish your seams, and then stuff the cover with your favorite duvet!

Reversible Duvet Cover Patterns

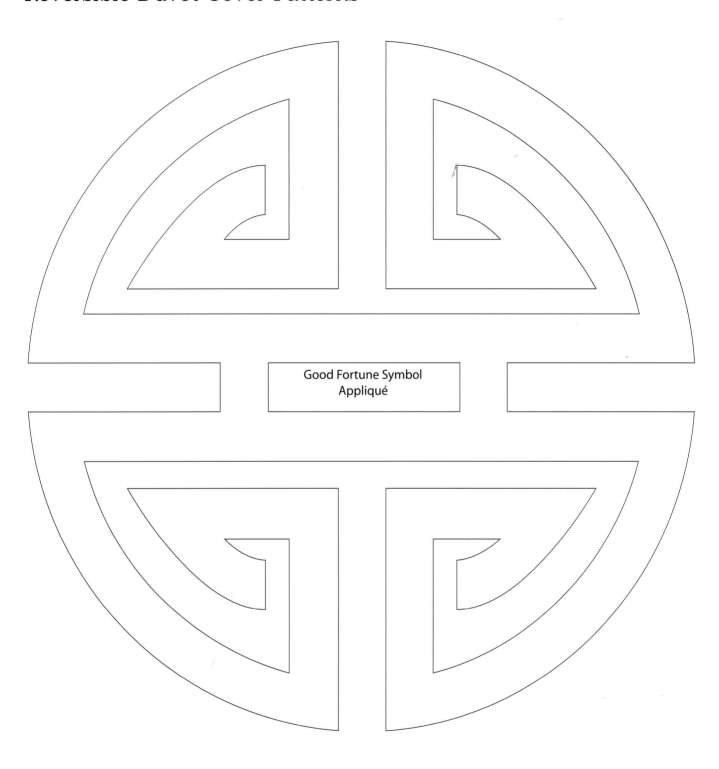

Good Fortune Symbol
Appliqué

Enlarge pattern 250% for actual size.

Reversible Duvet Cover Patterns

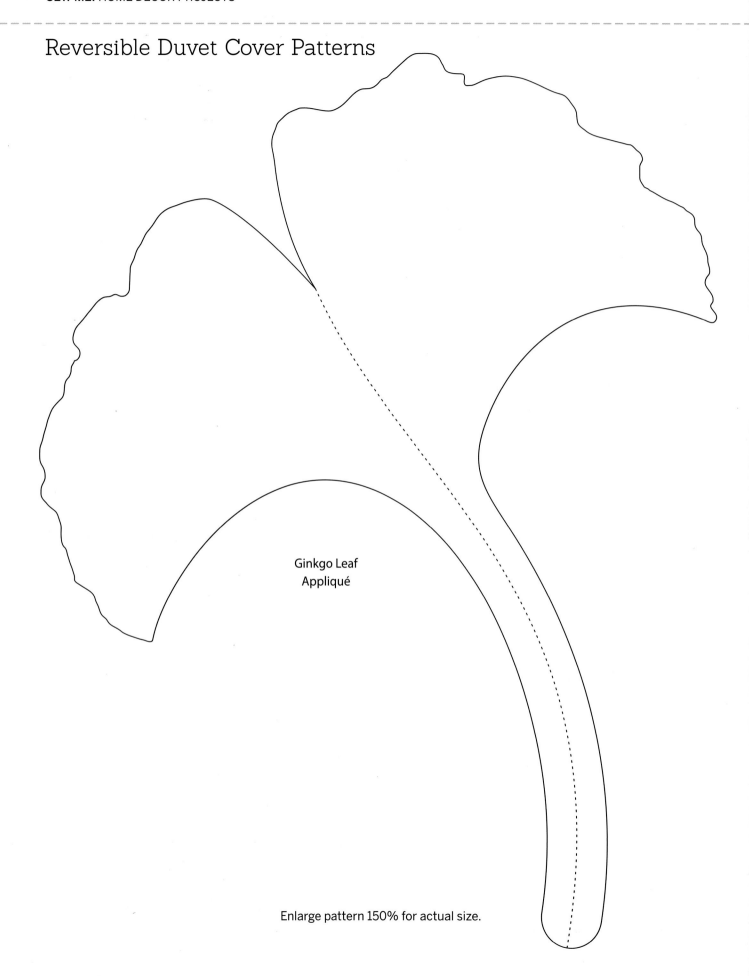

Ginkgo Leaf
Appliqué

Enlarge pattern 150% for actual size.

Cute Cube Storage Boxes

★★★★★☆☆☆

ESTIMATED TIME:
45–90 minutes

TECHNIQUES:
Appliqué, Interfacing

MAKES:
One 6" (18cm) cube

With all the wonderful notions, thread, and fabric you're buying, you're sure to have a lot of bits and bobs building up on your shelves. Give those items somewhere to go with this storage box. The process for this project has been made as simple as possible, while still ensuring you something useful and sturdy. And the optional cat, starburst, and thread appliqué designs will make your sewing studio as pretty as it is organized!

TIP: Be sure to use a needle for heavyweight fabrics to accommodate the heavyweight interfacing!

Materials

☐ ⅔ yd. (67cm) of light- to medium-weight woven fabric

☐ ⅔ yd. (67cm) heavyweight interfacing

☐ Five 5¾" (14.5cm) square pieces of cardboard, plastic sheeting, or ultra-firm interfacing (optional: see tip on page 68)

☐ Fat quarter or 10" x 10" (25.5 x 25.5cm) scrap of appliqué fabric (optional)

☐ 10" x 10" (25.5 x 25.5cm) square of fusible web (optional)

Tools

☐ Basic sewing kit (see page 25)

Your collection of fabric pieces for this project should look something like this:

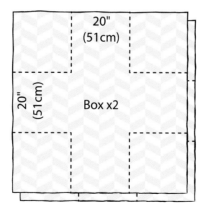

THE PREP WORK:

Cut your fabric pieces using the following chart, and any appliqué pieces from the patterns on page 69.

Storage Box Pieces

Piece Name	Material to Cut	Size to Cut	Number to Cut	Seam Allowance
Box	Light- to medium-weight woven	20" x 20"(51 x 51cm)	2	⅝" (1.5cm)
Box interfacing	Heavyweight interfacing	20" x 20"(51 x 51cm)	1	⅝" (1.5cm)
Appliqué design (optional)	Appliqué fabric and fusible web	To fit design	1	None

Cute Cube Storage Boxes *(continued)*

1 **Trim your box fabric.** Cut a 6¼" (16cm) square out of each corner of your box and interfacing pieces. You'll be left with a large + shape.

2 **Appliqué your design (optional).** See the Getting Started chapter (page 39) to choose a method for applying your decorative fabric to the box sides. Sew the appliqué at least 1" (2.5cm) in from the edge of the outer squares for the proper placement.

3 **Apply the interfacing.** Place the interfacing piece over the fabric piece that has the appliqué, lining up the edges. Following the manufacturer's directions, fuse the interfacing to the wrong side of the fabric completely.

4 **Fold the top edges.** For both fabric pieces, fold under the top edge of each square toward the wrong side by ⅝" (1.5cm). Iron these folds in place.

Experiment!

Try fusing some old grocery bags together (page 22) or laminating some colorful found objects for this project (page 24). Be sure to fuse several bags or laminate a thick medium so that you'll end up with a stiff material that doesn't need interfacing. In fact, after your box pattern is cut out, just sew up the sides as in Step 6, and you're done!

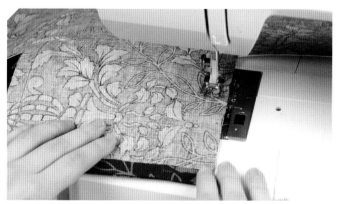

5 **Sew the inside to the outside.** Layer the box pieces together with right sides facing, and sew along each corner of the + sign, leaving the folded tops of the squares free. Clip the seam allowances, turn the fabric right side out, and press.

Cute Cube Storage Boxes *(continued)*

6 **Sew the sides.** Fold the box diagonally to match up the sides of two squares. Edge stitch the sides together about ⅛" (0.5cm) away from the seams. Repeat until all sides are sewn together and you have a box.

7 **Sew the tops.** Edge stitch along the top of the box about ⅛"–¼" (0.5cm) away from the folds.

Rock Solid:
GET MORE STABILITY FROM YOUR BOX

If you'd like a box with even more stability, insert squares of cardboard, plastic, or ultra-firm interfacing—anything that's firm, yet somewhat flexible.

Insert a square in the bottom. After Step 5, sew lines connecting the bottom corners of three of the squares (mark the lines to make it easier). Insert a square of cardboard, plastic, or ultra-firm interfacing cut to fit the bottom of the box into the fourth square and push it into place. Then, sew along the bottom of the fourth square, enclosing the bottom piece.

Insert squares in the sides. Continue through Step 6, but before Step 7, slide four squares cut to fit the sides of your box into the sides using the top openings. Continue with Step 7 and you have a much more stable storage box!

Cute Cube Storage Box Patterns

Mod Starburst
Appliqué

Thread
Appliqué

Cat
Appliqué

Patterns shown at actual size.

Ruffled Pillow Cover

★★★☆☆☆☆

ESTIMATED TIME:
45–90 minutes

TECHNIQUES:
Gathering, Hemming,
Measuring, Appliqué

MAKES:
One cover sized to match
your pillow

Materials

- ☐ Lightweight woven fabric in length D (rounded up to the nearest ¼ yd. [25cm] for insurance)

- ☐ Fat quarter of appliqué fabric (optional)

- ☐ ½ yd. (50cm) of fusible web (optional)

- ☐ **For ruffles:** Lightweight woven fabric in length G (for best results use very delicate wovens, such as gauze or voile)

Tools

- ☐ Basic sewing kit (see page 25)

- ☐ Safety pin

- ☐ Chopstick or similar turning tool

Find your style!

Search around for some men's button-down shirts at your local thrift store, and this pillow cover is as easy as it gets! Simply cut your pillow back and front from the middle of the shirt, centered over the button panel. Now you can jump right to Step 6, and the buttons serve as the new opening for your cover!

Go crazy with ruffles with this luxurious pillow cover. Whether you go with rows of gathers, a scattering of flowers, or maybe the included feather, leaf, or bellflower appliqué, you'll be decorating your home in no time, and it's so easy!

MEASUREMENTS

Work out these equations to find out what size pieces to cut. Feel free to round up to the nearest ¼" or 0.5cm for each final measurement to make things easier:

Pillow width + 1¼" (3cm) = _____ A (Cover width)

Pillow length + 1¼" (3cm) = _____ B (Cover length)

Pillow length × 0.6 + 1¾" (4.5cm) = _____ C (Back length)

C × 2 = _____ D (Cover yardage)

Pillow length × 2 = _____ E (Ruffle length)

Pillow width ÷ 5" (10cm) = _____ F (Number of ruffles rounded up to nearest whole number)

F × ¼ yd. (25cm) = _____ G (Ruffle yardage)

Measure the length and width of your pillow to determine the dimensions of your cover.

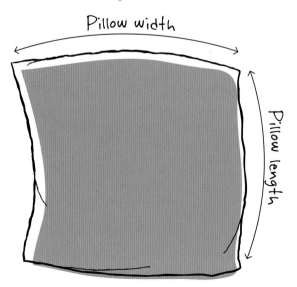

Pillow width

Pillow length

Ruffled Pillow Cover *(continued)*

Your collection of fabric pieces for this project should look something like this:

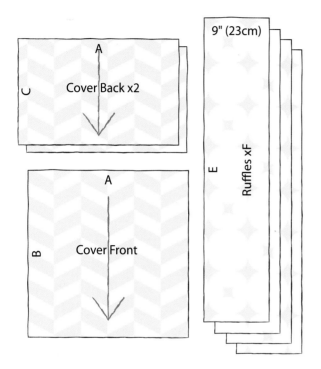

Experiment!

This is probably the ideal project for trying out new and unusual fabrics, especially if you keep it simple and skip the ruffles or flowers. Here are some things to try:

- Use knit fabrics for a pillow that feels extra squishy and huggable.
- Fleece makes for a cover that's comfy and warm.
- Satin fabrics (thick, stable brocades are ideal) instantly give your home a romantic boudoir feel.
- Minky fabrics are bright and colorful, but also luxuriously soft, perfect for a cozy movie night.

THE PREP WORK:

Cut your fabric pieces using the following chart, and any appliqué pieces from the patterns on pages 76–77.

Pillow Cover Pieces

Piece Name	Material to Cut	Size to Cut	Number to Cut	Seam Allowance
Cover front	Lightweight woven	A x B	1	⅝" (1.5cm)
Cover back	Lightweight woven	A x C	2	⅝" (1.5cm)
Vertical ruffles	Lightweight woven	9" (23cm) x E	F	½" (1.5cm)
Appliqué design (optional)	Appliqué fabric and fusible web	To fit design	1	None

Ruffled Pillow Cover (continued)

1 **Appliqué your design (optional).** See the Getting Started chapter (page 39) to choose a method for applying your decorative fabric to the cover front. Sew your appliqué on the center or at least 1" (2.5cm) in from the edges of the fabric.

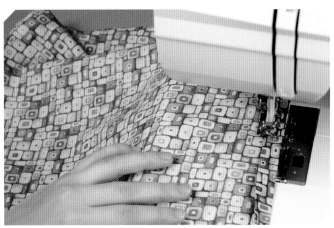

2 **Hem the back pieces.** Fold over one long edge of each cover back piece toward the wrong side by ⅝" (1.5cm) and iron it in place. Fold over the fabric by ⅝" (1.5cm) again and iron it. Sew this fold in place near the edge to create the double-fold hem.

3 **For a ruffle pillow: Prepare the ruffles.** Fold each ruffle piece in half lengthwise with right sides facing, and sew down the open long edge using a ½" (1.5cm) seam allowance. Turn the ruffles right side out with a safety pin and iron them with the seams in the center.

4 **For a ruffle pillow: Create the ruffles.** Sew a gathering stitch down the middle of each ruffle and create gathers in the fabric by pulling on the bobbin threads when finished. Gather the fabric until the ruffles are the length of B (the cover front length).

Experiment!

When you've had some practice with knits, try making the ruffles in soft cotton jersey. The edges can be left raw, so cut the strips half as wide and skip Step 3. With some practice, you'll have a snuggly pillow with a fresh boutique style!

Ruffled Pillow Cover (continued)

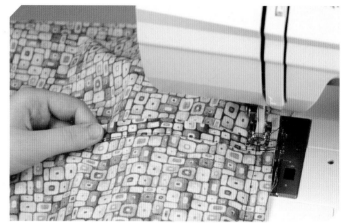

5 **For a ruffle pillow: Apply the ruffles.** Mark lines horizontally across the right side of your pillow cover front to mark the placement of each ruffle. To evenly space the ruffles, you'll find the lines should be about 5" (12.5cm) apart. Lay your ruffles over the lines and sew them to the right side of your cover front, stitching along the center of each ruffle.

6 **Complete the cover.** Layer the cover back pieces on top of the cover front with right sides facing. Align the back pieces to the top and bottom edges, and the middle hemmed edges will overlap. Sew along the entire perimeter of the case. For a ruffled pillow, be sure not to accidentally catch the ruffles when sewing the sides, but you will sew over them when stitching along the top and bottom. Trim the seam allowances, finish the seams, turn the case right side out, and poke the corners with a chopstick for more definition.

A Field of Flowers

Create flowers to cover your pillow by following the directions on page 75. Sew as many or as few as you'd like, and then use a ladder stitch to apply them to the cover front before completing the cover.

Apply ruffled flowers.

Creating Gathered Flowers

Materials

☐ ⅛ yd. (12.5cm) of lightweight woven fabric

Tools

☐ Basic sewing kit (see page 25)

These flowers are super quick to make and can be used to embellish any project you choose. I like to add them to the fronts of pillow covers for a special decorative touch.

THE PREP WORK:
Cut an 18" x 3" (45.5 x 7.5cm) strip of fabric.

Your fabric pieces to create a flower should look something like this:

3" (7.5cm)	18" (45.5cm)
	Fabric Flower

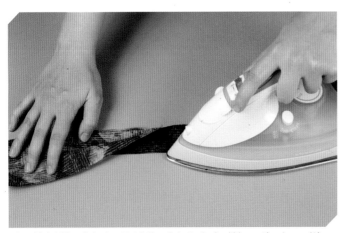

1 **Fold the fabric.** Fold the fabric in half lengthwise with wrong sides together and iron it flat.

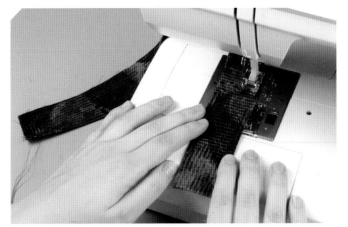

2 **Sew the gathering stitches.** Using a gathering stitch, sew completely around the raw open edges of the rectangle: the side, bottom, and then the other side. Do not sew the folded edge.

Creating Gathered Flowers (continued)

3 **Gather the fabric.** Begin gathering the fabric by pulling on the bobbin threads. Stop when the fabric measures 6" (15cm) long.

4 **Shape the flower.** Roll the fabric around itself to form a pinwheel and make the flower shape. Hand sew several knots that wrap around the bottom of the flower to hold the gathers in place. Using a ladder stitch, attach as many flowers to your pillow cover front as desired.

Ruffled Pillow Cover Patterns

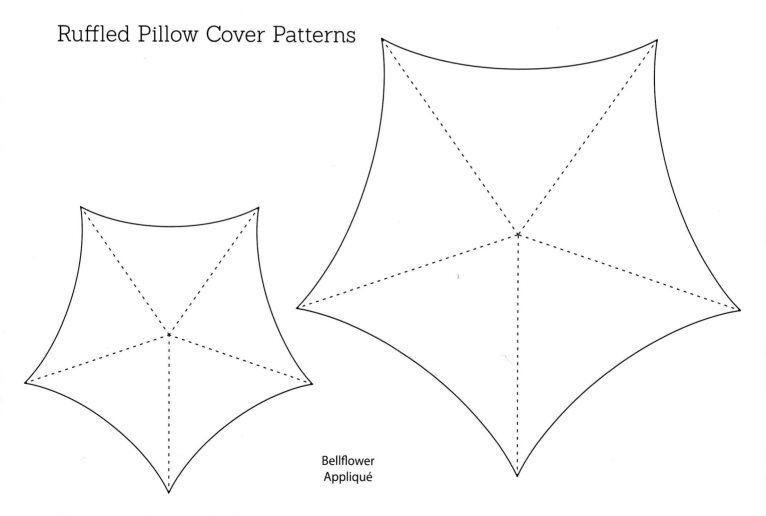

Bellflower
Appliqué

Enlarge patterns 125% for actual size.

Ruffled Pillow Cover Patterns

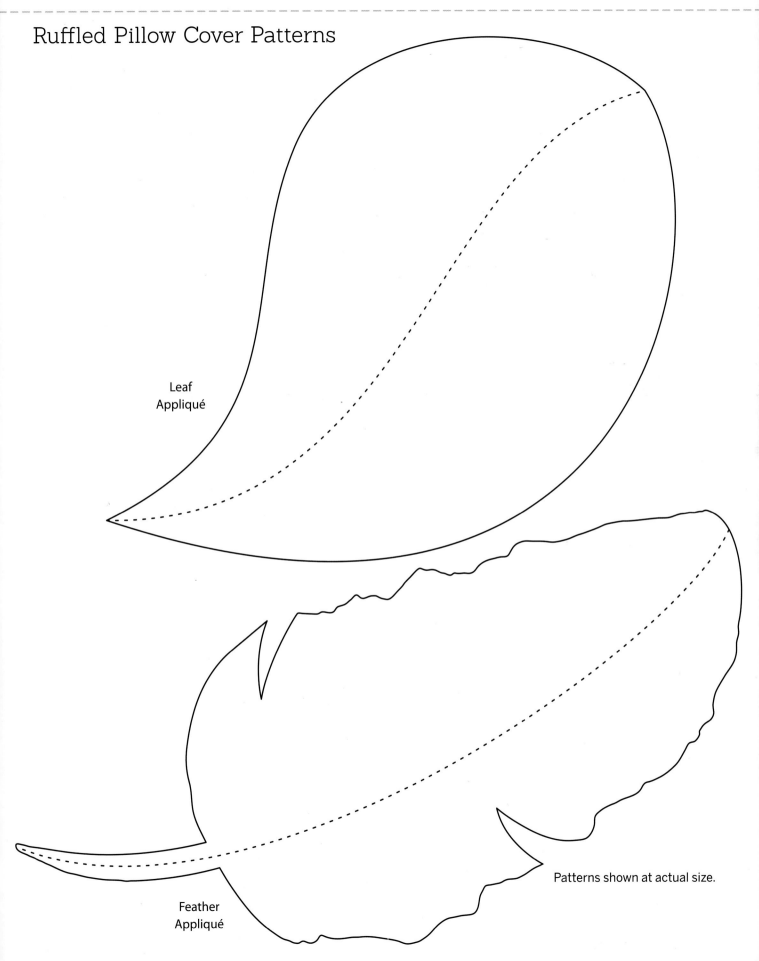

Leaf
Appliqué

Feather
Appliqué

Patterns shown at actual size.

Modernist Quilt

★ ★ ★ ★ ★ ★ ★ ★

ESTIMATED TIME:
6–12 hours

TECHNIQUES:
Binding

MAKES:
One 46" x 46" (117 x 117cm)
throw quilt

Materials

- ☐ 1⅓ yd. (133cm) quilting cotton
  in color A—front (black)

- ☐ 1⅓ yd. (133cm) quilting cotton
  in color A—back (black)

- ☐ 1¼ yd. (125cm) quilting cotton
  in color B—front (white)

- ☐ 1¼ yd. (125cm) quilting cotton
  in color B—back (white)

- ☐ ¼ yd. (25cm) quilting cotton
  in color C—front (blue)

- ☐ ¼ yd. (25cm) quilting cotton
  in color C—back (pink)

- ☐ Fat quarter of quilting cotton
  in color D—front (red)

- ☐ Fat quarter of quilting cotton
  in color D—back (orange)

- ☐ ¼ yd. (25cm) quilting cotton
  in color E—front (yellow)

- ☐ ¼ yd. (25cm) quilting cotton
  in color E—back (purple)

- ☐ 2¼ yd. (225cm) of 45" (114.5cm)-wide
  or 1⅔ yd. (167cm) of 60" (152.5cm)-wide
  fleece (thin is preferable) in white
  for batting

Tools

- ☐ Basic sewing kit (see page 25)

If you've ever thought quilts are too hard for a beginning sewer, think again! With the super simple quilt-as-you-go method, even large quilts like this one are within your reach. This method works from the middle of the quilt outward, making it easy to handle the large size. This technique works beautifully with simple strip designs, and the nature of the method makes the quilt reversible! Choose complementary or completely different fabrics for each side to create a totally different look. A modernist design probably makes the best use of this method, with this version that emulates a Mondrian painting. Use the traditional primary color scheme or go custom with your own choices.

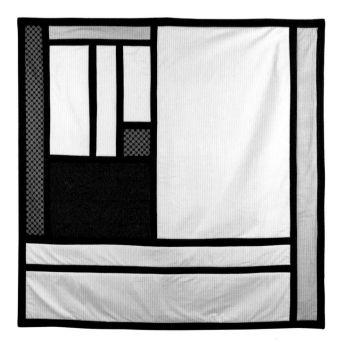

Modernist Quilt *(continued)*

THE PREP WORK:

Cut your fabric pieces using the following chart:

Quilt Pieces

Piece Name	Material to Cut	Size to Cut	Number to Cut	Seam Allowance
A1	Color A (black) for FRONT & BACK plus FLEECE	2" x 5" (5 x 12.5cm)	1	½" (1.5cm)
A2		2" x 17" (5 x 43cm)	2	½" (1.5cm)
A3		2" x 16" (5 x 40.5cm)	2	½" (1.5cm)
A4		2" x 32" (5 x 81.5cm)	2	½" (1.5cm)
A5		2" x 41" (5 x 104cm)	2	½" (1.5cm)
A6		2" x 45" (5 x 114.5cm)	3	½" (1.5cm)
A7		2" x 46" (5 x 117cm)	2	½" (1.5cm)
Binding	Color A (black)	3½" x 196" (9 x 498cm)	4	½" (1.5cm)
B1	Color B (white) for FRONT & BACK plus FLEECE	5" x 12" (12.5 x 30.5cm)	1	½" (1.5cm)
B2		4" x 17" (10 x 43cm)	1	½" (1.5cm)
B3		7" x 17" (18 x 43cm)	1	½" (1.5cm)
B4		21" x 32" (53.5 x 81.5cm)	1	½" (1.5cm)
B5		4" x 41" (10 x 104cm)	1	½" (1.5cm)
B6		9" x 41" (23 x 104cm)	1	½" (1.5cm)
C1	Color C for FRONT (blue) & BACK (pink) plus FLEECE	5" x 5" (12.5 x 12.5cm)	1	½" (1.5cm)
C2		4" x 32" (10 x 81.5cm)	1	½" (1.5cm)
D1	Color D for FRONT (red) & BACK (orange) plus FLEECE	12" x 16" (30.5 x 40.5cm)	1	½" (1.5cm)
E1	Color E for FRONT (yellow) & BACK (purple) plus FLEECE	3" x 16" (7.5 x 40.5cm)	1	½" (1.5cm)
E2		4" x 45" (10 x 114.5cm)	1	½" (1.5cm)

Modernist Quilt *(continued)*

Your collection of fabric pieces for this project
should look something like this:

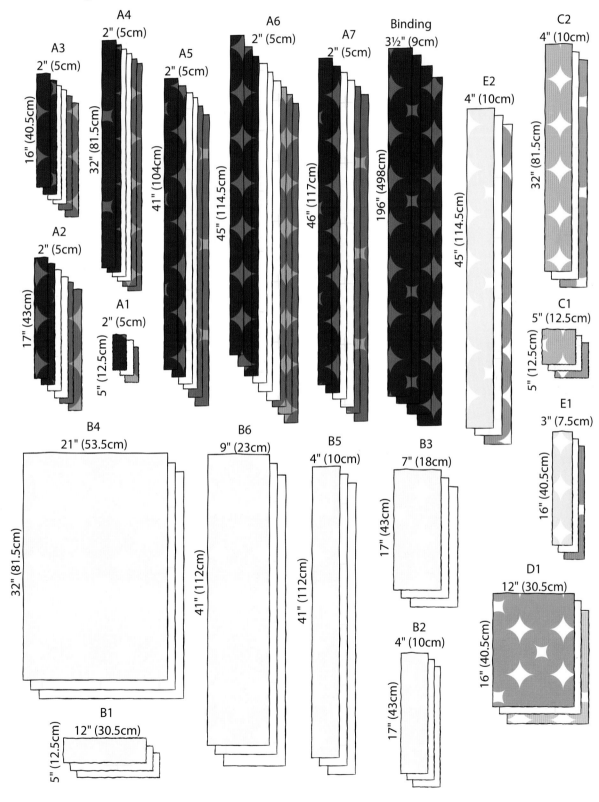

Modernist Quilt *(continued)*

For help while assembling, refer to this image as you go.

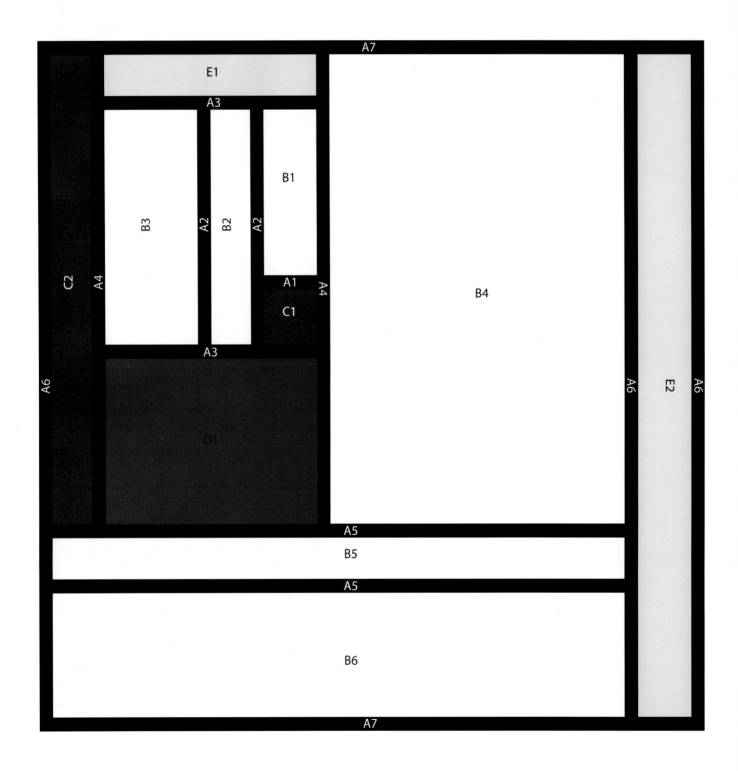

Modernist Quilt *(continued)*

1 **Layer the center of the quilt.** Gather all your C1 pieces: fleece, back, and front. With wrong sides together, sandwich the fleece between the cotton pieces, aligning the edges. Gather all your A1 pieces. Layer the front A1 piece over the front C1 piece with right sides facing, aligning the edges. Then layer the fleece over that. Layer the back A1 piece underneath.

2 **Sew the center of the quilt.** Sew completely along the edge to join A1 and C1. Then, fold the fabric away and press the seam. This is the quilt-as-you-go method and every seam for the quilt is completed like this. Repeat this by sewing the B1 pieces onto A1.

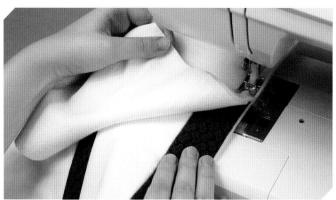

3 **Complete the center.** Layer the first set of A2 pieces over the long left edge of your work and sew them in place. Continue working outward with pieces B2, the second set of A2 pieces, and the B3 pieces.

4 **Begin the corner.** Layer the A3 pieces on the top and bottom edges of your work and sew. Continue moving outward with E1 on the top and D1 on the bottom.

5 **Finish the corner.** Layer the A4 pieces on the left and right edges of your work and sew. Continue moving outward with C2 on the left and B4 on the right.

Modernist Quilt (continued)

6 **Finish the bottom.** Layer the first set of A5 pieces on the bottom edge of your work and sew. Continue moving downward with B5, the last A5 pieces, and B6.

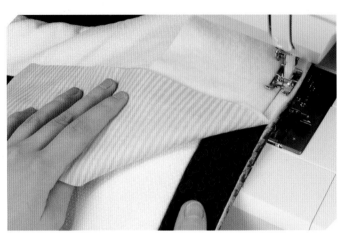

7 **Finish the side.** Line up the first set of A6 pieces on the right side of your work. Continue moving right with E2.

8 **Sew the borders.** Line up the last two sets of A6 pieces on the left and right and sew in place. Line up the two sets of A7 pieces on the top and bottom and sew in place.

9 **Bind the quilt.** Follow the binding instructions on page 85 to bind the edges of your quilt with the binding fabric.

Oops!

Try as you might, it can be hard to get all of your fabric edges perfectly lined up after every ironing, especially as your quilt gets bigger. If it's gotten bad, you can usually get away with trimming the uneven edges. Just make sure you trim parallel to the other lines of the quilt. Your finished project will be a little smaller, but it means you don't have to give up!

Bound with Style: Binding

Like hemming and pinking, binding is another way of finishing edges, but it does so with much more style. Because you're wrapping a raw edge with another fabric, you can choose whatever fabric you want for a snazzy contrast. For a beginner's introduction, we'll be applying a mitered binding made from vertical and horizontal strips of your favorite fabric. It takes some time to get used to, but once you understand the concept you'll be surprised how easy it is!

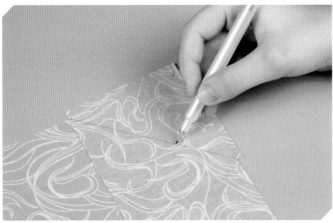

1 Make one long strip. Your pattern will indicate how long and wide your binding needs to be. Because it needs to be one continuous strip to cover your entire project edge, there's a good chance you won't have enough fabric to make the full length. To connect your pieces to make one long strip, line up the corners of the ends so they are at a 90° angle. Draw a line connecting the upper left corner to the lower right corner.

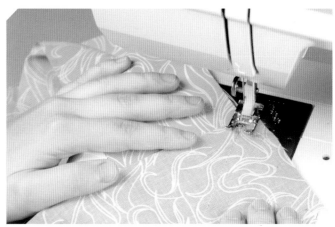

2 Chain the pieces. Sew along this line to create a diagonal connection between strips; your strip now won't have a huge bump where the seam was made like it would have if you had connected the edges vertically. Trim away the excess fabric and press the seam open.

3 Iron the binding. Fold the binding in half lengthwise with wrong sides together, matching the raw edges. Iron the entire piece in half.

4 Begin the binding. Line the raw edge of the binding up against the middle of the edge of your project from the right side. Start 6" (15cm) down from the end of your binding and begin sewing, using the suggested seam allowance.

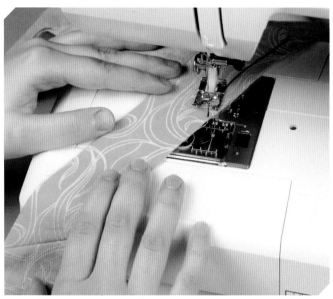

5 **Begin the corner.** When you come to a corner, stop before you get to the edge at a distance equal to your seam allowance. Pivot your work and sew off the edge of your project at a diagonal.

6 **Finish the corner.** Fold your binding back at a diagonal, away from your project, then fold it back toward your project, lining up with the raw edge of your project as before.

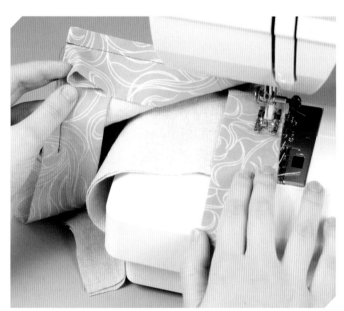

7 **Continue attaching the binding.** Prepare to sew the next side. Start your seam at the very top of the edge and back tack frequently so the seam is strong. Continue attaching the binding along the new side, and repeat steps 5 and 6 to create the other corners.

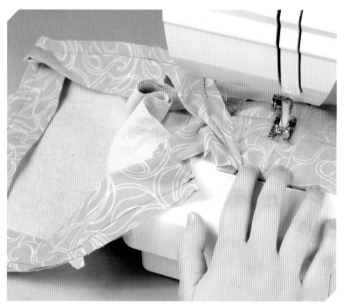

8 **Connect the ends.** Stop about 6" (15cm) before you reach your ending point. Open up the binding folds and line the ends of the binding up so that they are flush against your project. Mark this line, then sew them together along the line. Trim the seam allowance and press the seam open.

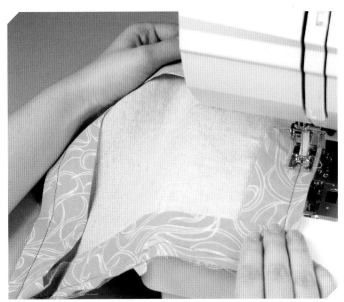

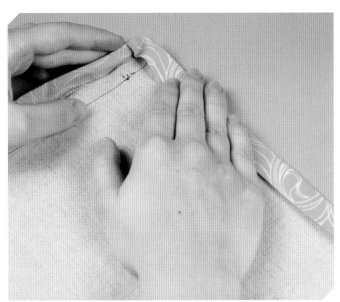

9 **Sew the last of the binding.** Smooth out your binding so the gap edges line up with the edges of your project. Sew this gap to complete the circle. Iron the binding away from the project.

10 **Wrap the binding.** Wrap the binding around the edge of your project toward the wrong side and fold the corners like an envelope. Pin and iron this in place.

11 **Sew the binding in place.** From the right side of the project, stitch in the ditch of the previous seam. Your stitching will be less obtrusive and if done properly it should catch the edge of the binding from the other side. Flip your work often to make sure this is happening.

Curtains for Window or Shower

★★★★★★☆☆

ESTIMATED TIME:
1–2 hours

TECHNIQUES:
Interfacing, Grommets, Hemming, Finishing Seams

MAKES:
One curtain sized to match your shower/window

Truly customize your living space with these easy curtains! Create one that's panel style or with big ruffles for a dramatic look. Add some accent color with the included appliqué patterns for leaves, butterflies, or raindrops.

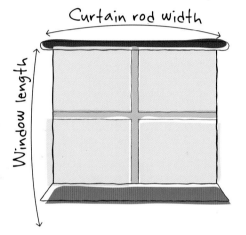

Measure the length of your window and the width of your curtain rod to determine the size of your window curtain.

Measure the length of your shower and the width of your shower rod to determine the size of your shower curtain.

MEASUREMENTS

Work out these equations to find out what size pieces to cut. Feel free to round up to the nearest ¼" or 0.5cm for each final measurement to make things easier.

Curtain rod width* + 4" (10cm) = _____ A (Curtain width)
*For a ruffled curtain, multiply the curtain rod width by 2

Shower length + 9" (23cm) = _____ B (Shower curtain length)

Window length + 12" (30.5cm) = _____ B2 (Window curtain length)

If your fabric is narrower than your rod width, you'll need to sew three panels together to create your full width. Follow these equations to calculate them:

Fabric width – Selvedges (cut them off) = _____ C (Center panel width)

For the side panel width:

Take C and subtract 1¼" (3cm) from it = _____

Take A and subtract your solution above from it = _____

Take this new number and divide it by 2 = _____

Take this new number and add 1¼" (3cm) to it = _____ D (side panel width)

Curtains for Window or Shower (continued)

Materials

- ☐ Light- to medium-weight woven fabric in lengths equal to B for a shower curtain or B2 for a window curtain (for three-panel curtains, you will need three lengths of B or B2)

- ☐ **Shower curtain:** ½ yd. (50cm) of lightweight fusible interfacing

- ☐ 1" (2.5cm) metal grommets, enough for each shower ring for your curtain

- ☐ Fat quarter of appliqué fabric (optional)

- ☐ ½ yd. (50cm) of fusible web (optional)

Tools

- ☐ Basic sewing kit (see page 25)

- ☐ Grommet setting tools (if applicable)

Your collection of fabric pieces for this project should look something like this:

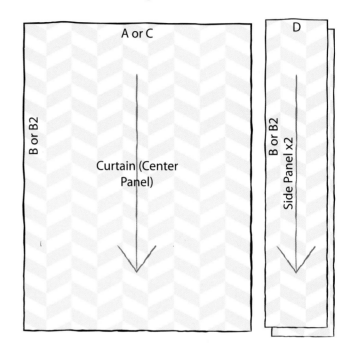

THE PREP WORK:

Cut your fabric pieces using the following chart, and any appliqué pieces from the patterns on pages 92–93.

Curtains Pieces

Curtain Type	Piece Name	Size to Cut	Number to Cut	Seam Allowance
Shower	Curtain	A x B	1	NA
Window	Curtain	A x B2	1	NA
Three-panel Shower or Window Curtain	Center Panel	C x B or B2	1	⅝" (1.5cm)
	Side Panels	D x B or B2	1	⅝" (1.5cm)
Appliqué design (optional)	Appliqué fabric and fusible web	To fit design	1	None

Curtains for Window or Shower (continued)

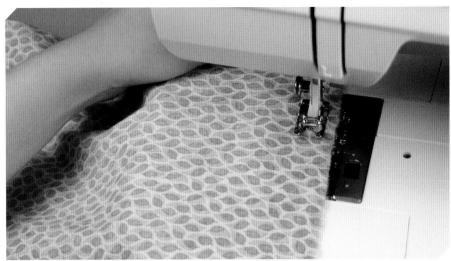

> **Tip**
> Be sure to measure your folds constantly while you make the hems so the edges look perfectly straight!

1 **Sew the curtain panels.** If your curtain needs to be sewn in three panels, sew a side panel to each side of the center panel along the long edges. Finish the seams and press them open.

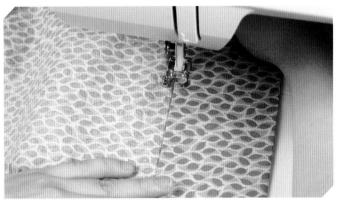

2 **Hem the bottom.** Fold under the bottom of the curtain to the wrong side by 2" (5cm) and press the fold. Fold under the bottom by another 4" (10cm) and press it flat. Sew close to this folded edge to create a double-fold hem.

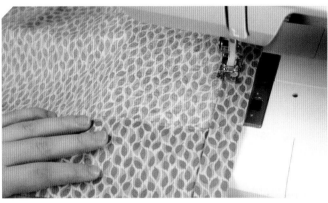

3 **Hem the sides.** Fold under the sides of the curtain toward the wrong side by 1" (2.5cm) and press the fold. Fold under the sides by another 1" (2.5cm) and press them flat. Sew close to these folded edges to create a double-fold hem along each side.

4 **Hem the top.** If you are making a window curtain, repeat Step 2 with the top of your curtain. This will create your rod casing. For a shower curtain, fold under the top of the curtain toward the wrong side by 1" (2.5cm) and press the fold. Apply a 2" (5cm) strip of interfacing across the top of the folded edge. Fold under the top by another 2" (5cm) and press the fold. Sew close to this folded edge to create a double-fold hem.

Curtains for Window or Shower *(continued)*

5 **Appliqué your design (optional).** See the Getting Started chapter (page 39) to choose a method for applying your decorative fabric to the curtain. Lay your fabric on the floor for the proper placement or fold it into quarters to find the center.

6 **Install the grommets.** Distribute the grommet markings across the top of the curtain, one for each shower hook. You can do this by measuring the width of your finished curtain, dividing this number by the number of shower hooks you have, and subtracting one. The number you get should be the length between each grommet while keeping one at each end of the curtain. Install the grommets at these points.

Curtains for Window or Shower Patterns

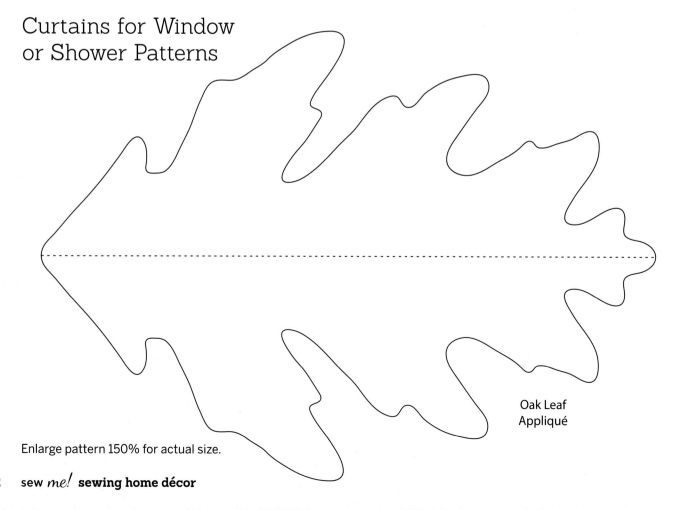

Oak Leaf Appliqué

Enlarge pattern 150% for actual size.

Curtains for Window or Shower Patterns

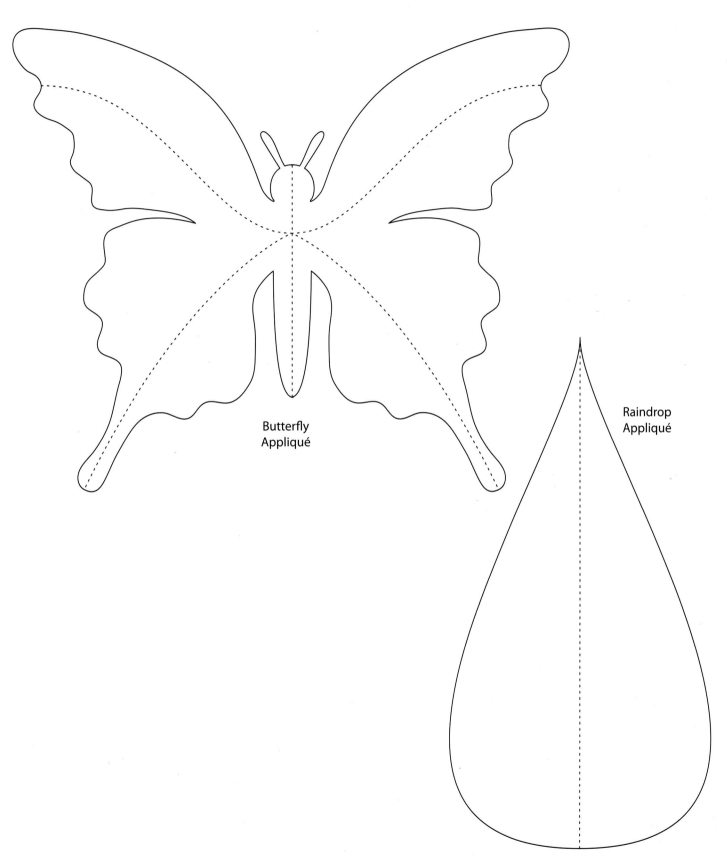

Butterfly Appliqué

Raindrop Appliqué

Enlarge patterns 150% for actual size.

Index

Note: Page numbers in *italics* indicate projects/patterns.

More Great Books from Design Originals

Sew Me! Sewing Basics
ISBN 978-1-57421-423-9 **$19.99**
DO5394

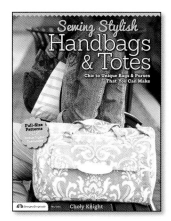

**Sewing Stylish
Handbags & Totes**
ISBN 978-1-57421-422-2 **$22.99**
DO5393

Sew Baby
ISBN 978-1-57421-421-5 **$19.99**
DO5392

Sew Kawaii!
ISBN 978-1-56523-568-7 **$19.95**

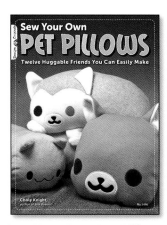

Sew Your Own Pet Pillows
ISBN 978-1-57421-343-0 **$8.99**
DO3466

Sewing Pretty Little Things
ISBN 978-1-57421-611-0 **$19.99**
DO5301

Soft Toys
ISBN 978-1-57421-501-4 **$9.99**
DO5422

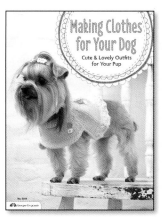

Making Clothes for Your Dog
ISBN 978-1-57421-610-3 **$19.99**
DO5300

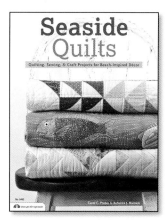

Seaside Quilts
ISBN 978-1-57421-431-4 **$24.99**
DO5402